UP TO MAMETZ

UP TO MAMETZ

BY

Ll. WYN GRIFFITH

GLIDDON BOOKS
NORWICH, NORFOLK

This 1988 edition published by
GLIDDON BOOKS

First published in the U.K.
1931 by Faber & Faber Ltd.

Reissued in 1981 by
Severn House Publishers Ltd.

ISBN 0 947893 08 3

Printed in Great Britain by
Biddles Ltd. of Guildford

TO THE MEMORY OF

PRIVATE WATCYN GRIFFITH

ROYAL WELSH FUSILIERS

'. . . . . . . i ddwys goffau
Y rhwyg o golli'r hogiau.'

INTRODUCTION

In April 1931, under the heading 'And Yet Again', an anonymous reviewer in *The Times Literary Supplement* surveyed the latest clutch of war books, Wyn Griffith's *Up to Mametz* among them. 'Publishers tell us that War-books are "done for",' he wrote, 'but continue to bring them out. Presumably they pay their way, but it is hardly probable that their sales are as great as a year ago. This is unlucky for the authors, for in many cases the books appearing now are superior to predecessors which had very great success. Of the six before us . . . four have merit, three of them considerable literary merit.' *Up to Mametz* is included in the three of greatest merit, and the comparison of these with their successful predecessors is high praise indeed, for their publication followed hard on the heels of Frederic Manning's *Her Privates We* and Siegfried Sassoon's *Memoirs of an Infantry Officer* (1930), Robert Graves's *Goodbye to all that* (1929), and Edmund Blunden's *Undertones of War* (1928).

By an accident of timing therefore *Up to Mametz*, though well reviewed and well received by readers, failed to achieve the level of success that it deserved. It sold about a thousand copies, then lay neglected until more recent times. For this Wyn Griffith blamed himself. Immediately after the war he had begun to write an account of his war service, but then lost interest and stopped after a few thousand words. When he came across the manuscript later he was horrified to find that he had so little to say about the greatest experience of his life. He started again by trying to remember what he felt and did on one single day. He began with a day in Givenchy, found that he remembered a lot, and kept on writing. What emerged is seen today as one of the classic books of the war: elegantly written (as might be expected of one who in later life was to help Sir Ernest Gowers hammer out *Plain Words*); accurate as a record of one particular action in the war; honest and sincere in intent; and, in the great climax describing the attack on Mametz Wood, in which his younger brother was killed, one of the most vivid and moving accounts ever written of the terrible experiences of war. Wyn Griffith however wrapped the manuscript in brown paper and put it back on the shelf for his children to read in later years. Only when a friend heard of it and read it did the process of publication begin. In recent decades, as the sixtieth and seventieth anniversaries of the Battle of Somme have come and gone, interest in the war has been rekindled and, in Wales at least, with the dedication of a memorial to the 38th (Welsh) Division at Mametz Wood in 1987, there is an increasing awareness of the sacrifices made in that particular attack. *Up to Mametz* was reprinted in 1981 with financial support from the Academi Gymreig, but copies of that edition are no longer available. This republication by Gliddon Books is therefore to be welcomed.

* * *

Llewelyn Wyn Griffith was born into a Welsh speaking family in Llandrillo yn Rhos in 1890 but most of his schooling took place in Blaenau Ffestiniog County School, where his father taught, and in the Grammar School at Dolgellau to which his father had moved on appointment as headmaster. He had every hope of going on to Cambridge but instead took the Civil Service examination and started work in September 1909 as an Assistant Surveyor of Taxes in Liverpool. The duties were not as grand as the title might suggest: copying, putting letters in envelopes, and gradually building up a knowledge of income tax in preparation for the departmental examinations on which his continued employment would depend; that was his day to day routine. If the work was uninteresting in itself, there were other compensations. The office was cheerful and Liverpool provided opportunities for a varied social life. It was there that he met the girl (also called Wyn) who was later to become his wife.

In the autumn of 1912 the Board of Revenue transferred him to London and he found his horizons suddenly widened. It was the golden period before the first world war, when everything seemed possible, and he threw himself into the cultural and political life of the capital city. His father came into a small inheritance and paid for him to become a student at the Middle Temple where he lived with several friends and read for the Bar while continuing to work for the Inland Revenue. He also began to write a little though he had no serious literary ambitions at the time. He attended the Friday evening salons at the house of Mrs. Ellis Griffith, wife of the Liberal MP for Anglesey, where the cream of the young Welsh in London talked, argued, drank coffee, listened to music, read plays and poetry. Here, Wyn Griffith came into contact with composers, dramatists, politicians and other influential people.

All this was shattered by the coming of the war. Wyn Griffith was on holiday in Dolgellau when war broke out in August 1914. On his return to London he found to his dismay that as a Civil Servant in the Revenue he was not allowed to join the armed forces. A little later, the rules were grudgingly relaxed to allow a few to join the newly formed Naval Division and, with a friend from his Liverpool days who had been active as an officer in the Naval Volunteer Reserve, Wyn Griffith promptly applied to join. The friend failed the medical and Wyn Griffith, refusing to join without him, decided that they should both try to enlist as privates in his county territorial battalion, the 7th Royal Welch Fusiliers. The medical examination in Newtown, Montgomery, turned out to be perfunctory and Wyn Griffith soon found himself with one stripe—an acting unpaid lance-corporal drilling other new recruits in Welsh.

Shortly before Christmas he heard from Mrs. Ellis Griffith that a battalion of the Royal

Welch Fusiliers—the 15th—was being raised in London and that he should apply for a commission. This he did and was accepted. In January 1915 he joined the battalion, which had moved to Llandudno, as a second lieutenant, commanding No. 10 platoon in C Company. The officers' mess was in the Grand Hotel on the pier and among the young officers billeted there Wyn Griffith found many friends from the Friday night salon.

The 15th (London Welch) Battalion was one of 12 infantry battalions in the 38th (Welsh) Division, which had been raised on the initiative of Lloyd George as his contribution to Kitchener's New Armies. The battalions were grouped into three brigades: the 113th, with four Royal Welch Fusilier battallions (13th, 14th, 15th and 16th); the 114th, with four battalions from the Welch Regiment (10th, 13th, 14th and 15th); and the 115th, with battalions drawn from all three Welsh regiments of the line (10th and 11th South Wales Borderers, 16th Welch, and 17th Royal Welch Fusiliers). Impressive though it looked on paper, the division, with a strength of more than 18,000 officers and men, was little more than a collection of raw volunteers, drawn from most parts of Wales and from the border counties, together with a mixture of Welsh exiles and Cockneys from London. Many of the senior officers owed their appointments to Lloyd George and were more versed in politics than in military matters. Such military experience as there was came from over-age officers and nco's 'dug-out' of retirement. Until the division left for France, regular officers and men were few and far between.

For the first half of 1915 the division was scattered along the northern coast of Wales, from Pwllheli in the west, where the artillery limbered up using old bus wheels and long poles for guns, to Prestatyn in the east. For months, the infantry drilled on the sea front and marched and marched. There was little else to do: the rifles issued to them had been condemned in 1902 and, perhaps wisely given the state of the guns, there was no ammunition. In August the division moved from north Wales to better training grounds at Winchester. The shortage of rifles and ammunition continued, however, until November when the division was told to prepare for embarkation. In the last few days in England each man fired about 24 rounds on the ranges at Salisbury Plain and was pronounced fit for battle. By then they were fairly smart and full of confidence. The War Office, however, was not so sure; some of the older officers were replaced by younger men, and some junior officers (Wyn Griffith among them) were sent on a short course in staff duties at Camberley. The War Office also recommended further training for the division in France.

* * *

Up to Mametz opens with the journey to France. Wyn Griffith has moved up to become second in command of C Company and has been gazetted in the rank of Captain—although he did not learn of his promotion until some time later, and in *Up to Mametz* chafes at the delay. The brigade to which the 15th RWF belongs has a new commander, 35 year old Brig-Gen Price-Davies VC, the 'second biggest fool' Wyn Griffith was to meet in four years of soldiering. The first part of the book describes C Company's apprenticeship in the front line at Christmas, and then tells of its experiences during six months of static warfare in Flanders, when the division occupied various parts of XI Corps' front, from Fauquissart (near Laventie) in the north to Cuinchy (on the La Bassée Canal) in the south. Although his perspective is necessarily limited by the nature of his duties as a company officer, Wyn Griffith very effectively conveys the amateurishness of it all: the drudgery, the dangers, the alternating sensations of boredom and fear, and the daily plague of visits from Price-Davies.

From June 1916 onwards, the perspective changes. The division marches south towards the Somme and the coming offensive. Wyn Griffith is detached from his battalion and brigade to take up duties in 115th Brigade headquarters, a move which he accepted with unconcealed escape, for it seemed to offer certain relief from danger. Circumstances, however, dictated otherwise. Although his position at brigade headquarters was a modest one—a temporary attachment for learning and general duties—he was soon in the centre of a storm. The brigade was chosen to lead the division's first attack in the Battle of the Somme, indeed its first offensive action of any kind. In the course of it the Brigade Major and the permanent Staff Captain were put out of action and Wyn Griffith became the Brigadier's right hand man.

* * *

Comparison with battalion, brigade, divisional and Corps diaries shows that Wyn Griffith's evocative description of the capture of

Mametz Wood, with which the book ends, is also accurate, down to the last detail. It needs no analysis here, but some background to the operations at Mametz Wood may help the reader to understand the intentions behind the attack, and the part played in it by the Welsh Division.

When the offensive on the Somme began on 1 July 1916 the British confidently expected to break through the German lines and sweep north across the open ground beyond. In the event, the only success was on the southern part of the front where 18th and 30th Divisions captured their objectives around Montauban, and the 7th and 21st Divisions of XV Corps partially did so by capturing Mametz village and breaking the German front line west of Fricourt. That evening it was decided to consolidate these gains and then to capture the German second line at its nearest point on the ridge between the Bazentins and Longueval. Rawlinson, in command of Fourth Army, planned a frontal assault on the ridge, with Mametz Wood on his left flank and another wood—Trones Wood—on his right. Haig intervened, however, to order the capture of Mametz Wood ahead of the main assault to protect the left flank.

Hammicks
BOOKSHOPS

Inspector Morse Competition

Death Is Now My Neighbour

Is The New Inspector Morse Novel And It Could Be Yours Simply By Entering This Easy Competition!

All You Have To Do Is Guess Morse's Christian Name - You Get Four Attempts....

Complete Your Entry Form With Your Name, Address And Telephone Number And Return It To; Hammicks Bookshop, 19 West Street, Horsham, Sussex RH12 1PB by Monday 9th September 1996.

1. ______________________ **2.** ______________________

3. ______________________ **4.** ______________________

Name: ____

Address: ____

____

Postcode: ___________________ **Telephone:** ___________________

Hammicks Bookshops
19 West Street, Horsham, Sussex RH12 1PB
Telephone 01403 268088 - Facsimile 01403 210536

Hammicks
BOOKSHOPS

Inspector Morse Competition

Death Is Now My Neighbour

Is The New Inspector Morse Novel And It Could Be Yours Simply By Entering This Easy Competition!

All You Have To Do Is Guess Morse's Christian Name - You Get Four Attempts....

Complete Your Entry Form With Your Name, Address And Telephone Number And Return It To; Hammicks Bookshop, 19 West Street, Horsham, Sussex RH12 1PB by Monday 9th September 1996.

1. ____________________ **2.** ____________________

3. ____________________ **4.** ____________________

Name: ____

Address: ____

____

Postcode: ____________________ **Telephone:** ____________________

Hammicks Bookshops
19 West Street, Horsham, Sussex RH12 1PB
Telephone 01403 268088 - Facsimile 01403 210536

Hammicks
BOOKSHOPS

Inspector Morse Competition

Death Is Now My Neighbour

Is The New Inspector Morse Novel And It Could Be Yours Simply By Entering This Easy Competition!

All You Have To Do Is Guess Morse's Christian Name - You Get Four Attempts....

Complete Your Entry Form With Your Name, Address And Telephone Number And Return It To; Hammicks Bookshop, 19 West Street, Horsham, Sussex RH12 1PB by Monday 9th September 1996.

1. ____________________ **2.** ____________________

3. ____________________ **4.** ____________________

Name: ______________________________

Address: ______________________________

____

Postcode: ______________ **Telephone:** ______________

Hammicks Bookshops
19 West Street, Horsham, Sussex RH12 1PB
Telephone 01403 268088 - Facsimile 01403 210536

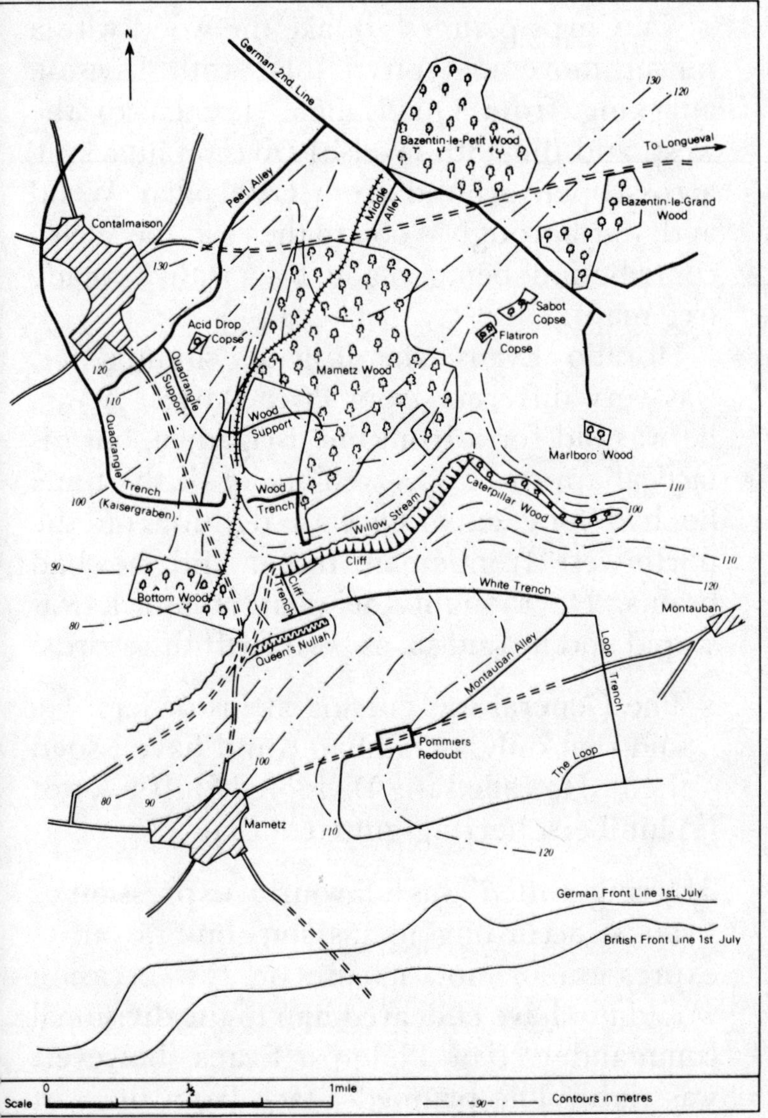

Mametz Wood and surrounding trenches

XV Corps planned to take the wood with a pincer movement on 7 July: 17th Division attacking from Quadrangle Trench to the west, and the 38th (Welsh) Division attacking across open ground from Caterpillar Wood and Marlborough Wood to the east, the Welsh contribution being made by 115th Brigade (see map).

Horatio Evans, the brigade commander, was very different from Price-Davies. At 55, he was old for a front line Brigadier, but his tactical approach was well ahead of the time, he had long experience of fighting on the north-west frontier in India, and he had brains. He thought the plan of attack was stupid and he said so, as Wyn Griffith records:

> The General was cursing at his orders. He said that only a madman could have issued them. He called the Divisional Staff a lot of plumbers, herring-gutted at that.

'Herring-gutted' was a favourite expression of Evans's, according to his son, but favourite expression or not, its use on this occasion would not have endeared him to the divisional commander, Ivor Philipps. Evans, however, was right. The planned attack from the east was not far short of suicidal: it was to be *parallel* to the German line and open to enfilade fire from Sabot and Flat Iron copses. Not surprisingly it failed. About 300 yards from the wood the Welsh attack petered out and the troops took whatever cover they could find. Casualties were high and attempts to reinforce were of no avail. Towards the end of the day, Brigadier Evans left his headquarters at Pommiers Redoubt and, taking Wyn Griffith with him, went down towards the wood to sort things out. He judged that the situation had become impossible, and using a field telephone found by Wyn Griffith, he persuaded the division to call off the attack. To the west, the 17th Division also failed to reach the wood. Wyn Griffith's initiative with the telephone may have saved some lives, or at least postponed some deaths, but it also contributed to the downfall of Ivor Philipps. On 9 July he was relieved of his position and the Welsh Division came under the temporary command of Maj-Gen Watts from 7th Division.

A second attack on the southern edge of the wood from White Trench was ordered for 10 July, the Welsh Division making the main thrust at 4.15 am using two brigades, the 113th on the left and the 114th on the right, with 17th Division assisting on the left flank. The plan had little subtlety, being a frontal attack over unpromising ground—down the cliff from White Trench then up the slope towards the wood. There were to be no feints, no outflanking manoevres. When the order to advance was given, three battalions moved down the cliff into a hail of shells and bullets with, as Wyn Griffith says, 'a success that astonished all who knew the ground'. The advance to the wood was made in good order, but once inside the wood thick undergrowth impeded progress. Shells from both sides hit the trees and detonations and splinters caused many casualties. Reinforcements were pushed in and the troops moved slowly through the wood. By about 11 am all eight battalions of the two brigades were involved in the fighting and two more, from 115th Brigade, were sent in to revive a flagging attack. The battle swayed to and fro but by half past six in the evening the division had reached to within 40 yards of the northern edge of the wood. To avoid close fire from the German second line, the troops were withdrawn 200 yards into the interior where they dug in for the night.

The following morning, Evans and his Brigade Major entered the wood to take command. While they were preparing for the next move forward, the Brigade Major was hit and Wyn Griffith, the novice of the staff, was sent to replace him. The rest of the story is told in *Up to Mametz.* Briefly, the fresh attack again took the division near to the far edge of the wood, but again it was forced to withdraw a little way to safety. But the Germans had had enough and that night—11/12 July—evacuated the wood leaving it in the hands of the exhausted Welsh. The 38th Division had driven the cream of Germany's army from the largest woodland on the Somme but Wyn Griffith's story does not end on a note of triumph. His brother had been killed carrying a message he had written. He had also witnessed the death and mutilation of men of his old battalion. With the other survivors he marched dejectedly away leaving behind 4,000 officers and men of the division dead or wounded.

A few days later, the Fourth Army captured the German second line on the Bazentin-Longuevel ridge. As it pressed on towards High Wood on the crest of the ridge, however, the Germans counter-attacked fiercely and brought the attack to a halt. High Wood remained in German hands for two more months. From that time forward, the Battle of the Somme became a battle of attrition.

* * *

After Mametz, the Welsh Division was withdrawn from the battle and sent northwards to a quiet part of the Somme front near Serre to recuperate and re-form. Brigadier Evans went back to England, never to return. Age, rather than any shortcomings in performance, prompted his retirement, but he thought otherwise and died a sad man.

With the brigadier gone, and other staff officers still not fit for duty, Wyn Griffith, still officially a learner, found himself the sole member of the brigade staff. One day the brigade received a visit of inspection from their new Corps commander. Wyn Griffith met him and saluted, and tried to explain who he was, and why he had no red tabs to distinguish him. The General interrupted him and said, 'You should say Captain Griffith, 15th Royal Welch Fusiliers, acting as Brigade Major and Staff Captain. Remember that! Do you know who I am? General Aylmer Hunter-Weston, commanding the VIII Corps. Take me to the field. Take a horse from my escort and ride by my side and tell me all about the brigade.' The General led off on a superb mount but Wyn Griffith's borrowed horse would not keep up with it. The General turned to him angrily and said, 'I asked you to ride with me, not behind me.' 'I'm sorry, sir,' said Wyn Griffith, 'but this horse has been trained to walk behind yours.' 'You are quite right. Never be afraid to give a good reason.' And with that the General inspected the brigade, made a speech and went away.

That was Wyn Griffith's first encounter with Hunter Bunter, as he was called behind his back. Towards the end of winter 1916/17, after a few detachments for staff training, Wyn Griffith was posted to VIII Corps General Staff, again on a temporary basis. It was not a happy place. Hunter-Weston was an exhibitionist, ambitious and erratic. Although a great talker he was never popular with his inferiors, equals or superiors. His Chief of Staff—Brig-Gen Ellington, later to become a Marshal of the Royal Air Force—had nothing but contempt for him. One of Hunter-Weston's least endearing characteristics was to give orders to junior officers (Wyn Griffith among them) designed more to impress those within earshot, than to achieve any worthwhile end. When this happened, Ellington would take steps to see that the orders were countermanded or ignored. Wyn Griffith found his visits to the trenches with Hunter-Weston an ordeal. The General, who had plenty of energy, would walk fast, criticise everything and everybody, and turn tired officers out of their dugouts. The better soldiers, Wyn Griffith noticed, despised him.

In May 1917 Wyn Griffith's fortunes took a turn for the better. Orders came for him to report to the General Staff of II ANZAC Corps at Bailleul where he was given a permanent appointment as GSO III. He was now a full-blown officer on a Corps Staff, with red tabs and cap band and an extra £400 a year in his pocket. The Corps was part of General Plumer's Second Army. Plumer was an enlightened commander, receptive to ideas from below. The Corps commander, Sir Alexander Godley, was also an excellent soldier, well thought of by his colleagues, and the staff was happy and efficient. In Plumer's masterly attack at Messines in June 1917 the Corps excelled itself, and the reputation of its staff grew. The Corps was afterwards given a roving commission and was sent to Passchendaele in October 1917 to try and pull things round. In the spring of 1918, renamed the XXII, it took over the sector north of Mount Kemmel, the last defence against the German advance to the Channel ports. Godley sent Wyn Griffith forward to find a dugout or strong point near a signal station to be the advanced Corps headquarters. From there, and with only one other staff officer present, Griffith watched Godley direct the battle. With 11 divisions at his disposal, and with maps and orders and reports before him, Godley moved brigades about, closed up reserves and took full responsibility upon himself to stop the German advance, a task in which he succeeded.

Wyn Griffith left the army in February 1919, three months after the war had ended. He never lost his admiration for the General Staff in the later stages of the war and regretted in later life that he had not written a second book to cover this stage of the war, not just to tell the story but to do justice to the commands and staff who were the targets for many of the published war books. Some aspects of this broader view can, however, be seen in *Up to Mametz*, where the memories of day-to-day events, so painfully recalled by Wyn Griffith in its writing, are overlaid with more mature thoughts. The shrewd comments he makes about the values and ingrained characteristics of the British army, are not the words of a young, inexperienced Company officer, but those of someone who has seen things from a higher vantage point. This is one of the strengths of *Up to Mametz*, and one that distinguishes it from many other war books. Few other writers saw the war from so many points of view: parade ground lance-corporal, company officer, staff captain in a prestigious Corps at the height of battle; few writers showed his understanding of the tragedy of war.

* * *

Wyn Griffith was mentioned in despatches for the part he played at Mametz, and was awarded the OBE (Military) and the Croix de Guerre in 1918. He returned to the Inland Revenue after the war, reached the grade of Assistant Secretary, and retired in 1952. He became Vice Chairman of the Arts Council, Chairman of the Council of the Honourable Society of Cymmrodorion, and held office in many other literary bodies. He was a noted broadcaster. He received the honorary degree of D.Litt from the University of Wales and was made a CBE in 1961.

Wyn Griffith died on 27 September 1977.

Sources

The biographical material in the introduction is taken from a section of an unpublished 'autobiography', written by Wyn Griffith in 1957 as a family record, and kindly provided by his son, Hugh Wyn Griffith. Other information is taken from Wyn Griffith's essay 'The Pattern of One Man's Remembering' in *Promise of Greatness*, [Ed] George A. Panichas 1968; from notes of my visits to Wyn Griffith in 1971 and 1972; from letters by Brigadier Evans's son, Peter Evans; from Greg Hill's *Llewelyn Wyn Griffith* in the Writers of Wales series; and from my own book *Mametz: Lloyd George's 'Welsh Army' at the Battle of the Somme*.

Colin Hughes
1988

CONTENTS

I

PRENTICE DAYS

PRENTICE DAYS

THE evening had declined into night without any perceptible change in quality. A heavy fall of rain had covered the streets with a thin grey film, reflecting the lights in the shop windows and silencing the tread of all who walked the pavements of Winchester in their last hours of freedom. There was so little that remained to be done, so much to say. Minutes of silence dragged their way through the dark places of the heart: speech sought a neutral path in a vague reassurance, avoiding the unreality of optimism and the sharp outline of despair. Some talk of leave and of the joy of meeting again, promises of letters, all in a coward's effort to avoid the challenge of the morrow and to escape from the unescapable. To the very end of the last hour, and through the ritual of parting, strength and safety lay in this determination never to give shape in words to the spectre of loneliness.

Throughout the night the rain fell heavily, turning the clay into a heavy mud. We struggled down the slopes of the downs, loaded with burdens that weighed on mind and matter, and in the early hours of the morning, marched for the last time through the streets of Winchester and along the road to Southampton.

The day passed without change of mood, in an even drive of wind and rain, into a late afternoon that found us on a wet quayside, staring at a grey ship on a grey sea. Rain in England, rain in the Channel and rain in France; mud on the Hampshire Downs and mud in the unfinished horse-standings in Havre where we sheltered from the rain during the hours of waiting for a train. Rain beating against the trucks as we doddered through an unknown land to an unknown destination, and, late at night, as we stood in the mud of a station yard near St. Omer, the rain was waiting for us, to drive us along twelve miles of muddy lanes to a sodden hamlet near Aire.

Four days out of England, days and nights of fatigue and stiff-limbed weariness, nights of little sleep and days of little rest: a hundred hours of rain. Little wonder that, for me, England had resolved itself into a vision of a white face looking out of a window in Winchester on a wet December morning, while France lay unrevealed behind this curtain of rain.

Next morning the world changed suddenly. We found ourselves in a flat country of pollarded willows and long poplars, red brick cottages with dark thatches, green meadows and roadside ditches, with a mild winter sun as the chief author of the change. The Army produced its unfailing remedy for all self-indulgence, its antidote against the fever of memory, in the shape of an immediate task.

At the back of our farmhouse was a stone-floored outhouse with a fireplace. A careful search in the cottages of the hamlet, and in the outlying farms, disclosed eight wooden wash-tubs, and after some negotiation, these were borrowed and carried into the outhouse. Three men of the company were told that so long as there was a continuous supply of hot water, they would be excused all parades. In an hour's time the enterprise was firmly established, and all day there was a steady changing of dirty men into clean men in clean clothes.

Next morning there came an urgent order from the Brigade that all ranks must have a bath and a change of underclothing. Worried Company Commanders were walking about the scattered hamlet in search of tubs, the Colonel was reputed to be cursing freely at the delay, but all in vain. 'C' Company had made a corner in wash-tubs. In the afternoon the Brigadier visited us, and his surprise at discovering that his orders had been forestalled by a Company officer was undisguised. Words of blame flow so easily down the slopes of rank, calling for no rehearsal, but giving shape to praise without implying excessive merit is a harder task. The stumble of phrases about the virtue of taking a personal interest in the comfort of 'the men' sounded somewhat unreal to a temporary officer who had but recently ceased to be a 'man'. I record the incident in a spirit of vanity mingled with amusement, for sixteen months of soldiering had been as barren of praise as they were rich in condemnation, and the 'bubble reputation' had come to me from soapsuds.

The days passed in uneventful succession, and the smaller matters of life grew into vivid importance as we adjusted ourselves to the routine of a new existence. Suddenly it became the fashion to crop one's hair. All the officers sat down in turn under the regimental barber's clippers. We had little claim to good looks before this drastic shearing, but all the villainy latent in our faces stood out naked after a prison crop. In our simple and childish eagerness we felt that by so doing we had made ourselves better fitted for the life before us, with its unknown hardships; we saw in this act some shadow of an initiation into the great mystery of the trench world, and we were somehow proud of it. How innocent it seems at this interval of time! It was to be followed soon after by a vigorous reaction, by a desperate striving to maintain every detail of personal pride in one's appearance. Had all the Army maintained this Spartan simplicity, the makers of brilliantine in France would not have enriched themselves so greatly at our expense.

One morning the battalion transport brought to our farmhouse a strange load from a source known vaguely as 'Ordnance'. Bundles of sheepskin jackets, white, grey and black, were thrown down at the side of the road. We wore them under our equipment, with the fur outside. They were designed to keep us warm in the trenches, but they grew so heavy when caked with mud that they gradually sank back along the road from the front, from the infantry to the mounted men, from them to the Labour battalions, until they faded away into the pit that engulfs the fashions of years gone by. They gave us the excitement of choosing the colour that pleased the most, and a slightly self-conscious strutting about the hamlet: we were matriculating.

Shortly afterwards we were hurled violently along our course. A solemn conference at battalion headquarters sent us back to our billets with a feeling that our quiet farmhouses were no more than a stone's throw from the front line. Gone was that sense of comfort and security, and darkness fell quickly upon that December day. Early next morning buses would arrive to take us to the front, in itself a simple event, but bringing in its train a multitude of small domestic cares and worries about billets, equipment, rations, orders and counter-orders that all but dwarfed into unreality the great transformation to be thrust upon us by the morrow. There was much to do before going to bed that night.

At eight o'clock on the morning of the 18th December, 1915, the company stood on parade in full marching order, pouches filled with ammunition, sheepskin jackets under the equipment, greatcoats rolled, and a cotton satchel containing a flannel gas-helmet slung over each man's shoulder. Half an hour later a fleet of London buses, painted grey, shook themselves clumsily along the muddy road. We mounted them with difficulty, fattened by our gear into unwieldy bundles, projecting rifles, entrenching-tool handles and mess-tins at unexpected corners of our bodies.

The morning passed quickly. We saw for the first time ammunition dumps, field hospitals, Ordnance workshops and Supply parks, every village bringing to our eager and excited minds some new embodiment of war. Outside Estaires we halted, on the La Bassée road. Here was a name we knew, part of the currency of war, and the very word, painted on a wooden signboard stuck on a house, seemed to throw us into contemporary history. In the moments that followed the impact of this new discovery, War suddenly came nearer to us, and thought would have travelled far but for the persistent intrusion of the task of the hour and place, the army's ancient cure for such indulgence. We dismounted and scattered ourselves along the roadside to eat our dinners of tinned stew—the unforgettable Maconochie.

The day was fine, and the sky clear of clouds. An aeroplane buzzed high up above us, with little white flecks appearing from nowhere and disappearing again. This was our first seeing of war and of the intent of one man to kill another. It was difficult to translate this decorating of a blue background with white puff-balls into terms of killing. Had we ever truly believed that our military training was a perfecting of our power to kill, that we were of no value to the world unless we were skilled to hurt? I do not think so. However soldierly our muscles might be, however willingly the body accepted war, the mind was still a neutral. Through all the routine of training we were treading a path planned by others, looking to the right and to the left, sometimes looking backwards with longing, but never staring honestly into the face of the future. This is the damnable device of soldiering: confronted with an unending series of new tasks, trivial in themselves and harmless, full of the interest associated with any fresh test of skill and endurance, tempting even in their novel difficulties, the young soldier is so concerned to triumph over each passing obstacle that he does not see the goal at the end of the race. No one persuades him that drill is an exercise, that marksmanship is but a weapon; to him they are not means, but an end. If he perceived from the start that skill in the fulfilling of these daily tasks was destined only to help him to kill his fellow man, there would be fewer soldiers. The antiquity of arms is nowhere shown more clearly than in this evidence of its long practice in the art of war and its close understanding of youth.

Here, on the La Bassée road, the battalion broke up into companies, and the companies into platoons. We were to be 'attached' to a brigade of Guards, to be taught by them the art and craft of trench life, and under the shelter of their greater responsibility we were to hold the line. The four platoons of my company were apprenticed to the four companies of a battalion of Coldstream Guards, so I marched off with a subaltern at the head of his platoon, guided by a Guardsman sent to meet us. Our masters were in reserve, scattered about in some ruined farmhouses a mile to the East of the La Bassée road. Falling dusk, flashes in the sky and the noise of guns, the stammer of machine guns, shell holes in the road, and a strange emptiness over the country, as if man had deserted it, all fused together into a gloom in the mind.

Some of the men turned off to a barn, and a little later we stopped at a group of battered cottages where my subaltern and I walked into a kitchen. This was the headquarters of the Guards company. The three officers greeted us in a manner benevolently neutral, showing neither cordiality nor resentment at the sudden burden of two thrown upon the company mess. Dinner followed, and a glass of port. What had we done to our hair? Why did we wear men's equipment and sheepskin coats? They smiled quietly, but not unkindly, at our answers, while we tried to learn as much about our task as question and answer could teach us. We were facing war, but they were turning away from it, tired in mind and body, as it seemed.

We slept upon some straw in an outhouse. I hesitated before asking whether I might take off my boots, but I was gravely assured that I might do so, as we were two miles behind the line. I was obsessed by the noise of our guns; they seemed to be firing over the cottage, shaking the floor and the walls. Through the broken corner of the roof I could see a star passing in and out through a dark cloud, and a distant rumble of transport brought a feeling that day and night were but arbitrary divisions of unending time; my period of rest was to another soldier the high noon of his activity. Thought swung uneasily from the known, with its clearly defined and pressing burden of practical worries, to the highly dramatized vision of the change that the morrow must bring into our lives. Less than twenty-four hours stood between us and the trenches; there were two kinds of men in the world—those who had been in the trenches, and the rest. We were to graduate from the one class to the other, to be reborn into the old age and experience of the front line, by the traversing of two miles over the fields in Flanders. Did one experience a sudden change of heart—would the fear of death overwhelm all else—could that fear be disguised, or must we suffer the humiliation of showing to others that for us, Time was standing still? These thoughts were but clammy companions on a dark night in a strange place: reason could not drive them away, but fatigue triumphed over all in the end and brought sleep.

The day passed in inactivity: we were not to walk about more than was necessary lest we provoke a shelling of this quiet byway. In the evening we paraded on the road, carrying on our backs sufficient tackle to provide for all emergencies in a march from Flanders to the Rhine. The Guards were not so cumbered, and their greatest anxiety was to run no risk of a lack of firewood. We dared not imitate them, for our orders were stringent, and their officers would encourage no departure from the letter of our law, however unwise they deemed it in the light of their greater experience. There was little talking: we were anxious, and they were bored. The roll was called, and we set off East in separated sections—Artillery formation, as it was called. Our destination was Fort Erith, a name that suggested a bastion fortified against all attack, to be held at every cost, wonderfully strong and secure, a key position, growing with every thought into an overwhelming importance as the pivot of England's struggle against Germany. So ran the mind as we marched along a narrow road with a low hedge on one side and a long-grassed moor on the other. The moon came out, and in its light we saw that the moor was only a derelict meadow. Lights were flashing in the Eastern sky, strangely high up in this flat country; that was Aubers Ridge, said my companion. We broke into single file. A singing note drooped through the air—what was that? A stray bullet. Another followed, and another, and the sound grew ominous to me. Were we not conspicuously outlined against a white road in this moonlight—could not the enemy see us? No, not at this distance: it was very rarely that any one was hit on this road. A sudden buzz of talking ahead, and the closer shuffling of our file showed that something had caught the attention of those who marched before us, bringing that slight slackening of pace that travels down the line like a concussion in a train of shunting trucks. Three men, and a stretcher lying on the roadside in the shadow of the hedge—a wounded Guardsman greeting us happily and inviting us all to share in his delight at his good fortune. The whine of the next spent bullet became malevolent and full of danger.

We stepped down into a communication trench, and although we were so much nearer the enemy, there was a sign of safety in these muddy walls. The duckboards underfoot were unevenly set and covered with a slimy layer of mud, the trench turned right and left in a maze of windings, here deep and there shallow. What was this peculiar smell, so persistent in its penetration that the mouth tasted of it? Why was I so thirsty? Suddenly we found ourselves pushing past other soldiers leaning against the wall of the trench; we were in Fort Erith. The moon came out again, and I saw a wet straggling trench with bulging sides, uneven fire-steps and ramshackle dug-outs. This was the bastion, the wonderful fort of my imagining! A child had begun to build this mud castle and had tired of his play—were men to fight for this thing? Did it rank as a strong point? Was this a part of England's defence?

We stooped through a narrow doorway leading into a dug-out, and before I had removed sufficient of my equipment to allow me to sit down, the formalities of handing over the command of the fort were finished. Two tired men were bidding each other good-night—how tired they seemed, tired in mind and jaded. A sackcloth curtain covered a small window, another made a *portière* across the door, and a new candle stood in its grease on the middle of the table. I studied a plan of the redoubt, while its commander gave orders to a sergeant. We were in the trenches, a little behind the front line, but where was the great change, the rebirth that was to follow this initiation? Why was I not afraid? I was thirsty, but in no other way different from the man who had imagined an upheaval in his whole way of thinking, a warping of his direction now and for ever. The great transformation that I had so dreaded in advance had dissipated itself into a sequence of minute experiences, each in its turn claiming a concentration that forbade any remembering of its predecessor. A heavy pack, a pitted road, uneven duckboards in a trench, the steering of an awkward body past the projecting walls and its balancing on a slimy foothold—this was the sequence of problems, large in their moment, that had overshadowed the greater ordeal, dwarfing it into the insignificance of a dream.

I followed my companion round the circle of our trenchwork, listening to his orders and absorbing as much as I could of his general attitude as he gave his quick answers to questions that appeared to me to be of great moment. Four men were to go outside the parapet to fill sandbags for the rebuilding of one bay; to leave the shelter of this ditch seemed a desperate venture, to stand on top of the parapet an unjustifiable challenge, but they thought nothing of it. I jumped down from the fire-step, glad of a buttress between me and the bullets that could not fail to sweep that parapet the next second—every second that passed in silence increased the possibility of danger in its successor, as I thought. I had stood for some minutes, head and shoulders exposed, in apparent unconcern, but seized with terror in anticipation of some calamity, and I did not attempt to ignore my secret relief at the end of this long waiting.

'This ain't so bad, this ain't,' I heard one of my men say. 'I wonder what it's like in the front line?' 'Wet,' answered a tall Guardsman.

'Rotten dug-outs.' He measured life on a scale of comfort and not according to the possibility of its extinction. Did one grow to rate comfort above safety? To me it seemed unbelievable that the edge of a desire for survival, so infinitely important to each individual man, could ever be dulled.

Dinner was ready; fried beef, boiled potatoes, and tinned fruit, followed by a cup of coffee and a glass of port. It was nearly ten o'clock, and I was hungry. Food brought with it a certain reinforcement, as if the mind had shared in the strengthening of the body; now I could believe that there was in reality a line of men between us and the enemy, that the night would not bring a sudden wild battle against a powerful foe. The three hundred yards that separated us from the front line became a measure of distance, not of nearness. I drew the Guards Officer into a discussion of the varying degrees of safety that characterized different parts of the line, in the hope of learning something of our own chance of safety; this was in reality but a disguising of my personal anxiety. I heard that the enemy rarely shelled this post unless our fires gave out too much smoke during the day.

The night was divided into three sections. From eleven until two we would keep joint watch, so that I might learn my duties; from two till four I was to take watch alone, and from four until stand-to the Guards officer would be on duty. We walked about as foremen of a building scheme, giving counsel here and criticism there. The night was quiet, and I learned the language of the various sounds of war—rifle-fire, machine-gun bursts, and light shell-fire, while from several points on the circumference of our post came the steady whack of a spade on the piled sandbags, rising from a dullish thud to a metallic and clear ring as the mud hardened beneath the blows. At two o'clock in the morning I was left alone to walk the decks of this vessel of war, proud of my responsibilities, but fearing to test either their extent or my powers of response. I walked from bay to bay, watching the men at work, overhearing strange and unfinished scraps of conversation from the dug-outs as I passed, content to be a presence, risking no exposure of my ignorance by any overt act of supervision. Time crawled, and the same thoughts recurred again and again—how long would this new life last . . . Wyn would now be fast asleep in Winchester . . . when would they gazette my captaincy and let me draw the extra five shillings a day, a windfall to a married subaltern . . . why did no one reset this sinking duckboard, by the very door of the dug-out?

At four o'clock I was to wake up my companion and to take my turn of rest, but when the time came I found a little pleasure in waiting, continuing my watch till half past four, and finding in this demonstration of a lack of haste a showing of my capacity to bear my burden. I turned into our dug-out and lit the candle, roused the sleeping Guards officer, and said that it was half past four; nothing had happened during the night. He got up slowly and stiffly, lit a cigarette and went out shivering. I stretched myself on the hard floor, making a pillow of my haversack, but I spent so much time trying to make myself comfortable, trying to keep warm, and trying not to listen to the noises of the night, that when somebody shouted 'Stand-to' I had nothing beyond a chill and aching stiffness in my legs to convince me that I must have slept. The dull grey dawn brought with it a greater intensity of cold and a hollow hunger. The garrison was stamping its feet in a lethargic attempt to remove the ache from its toes, some were swinging their arms or blowing upon their fingers, and all looked gaunt and grim. But of all the sights of that early December morning, the strangest was Fort Erith. A shabby, unfinished aggregate of mud, old sandbags, sagging posts and rusty wire, decayed and evil-looking, uneven parapets and bulging ramparts, pits of muddy water, stagnant and rank. A splintered stump of a tree trunk peered over the wall, ragged and black, a coil of barbed wire lay rusting on a fire-step, and an old ground sheet, torn and mud-stained, flapped stiffly against a staggered post. Grey desolation everywhere, till it was hard to believe that the garrison was alive. This mean ditch a fort? It was incredible that our lodging, with its appearance of a hastily improvised and quickly abandoned earthwork, should masquerade as a strong point in a system of defences. As the light became stronger, its imperfections grew out of a mass of detail into a total inadequacy of protection or of shelter; security and comfort were impossible of attainment. Surely the front line trenches were stronger and better planned, or else we had little safety!

We stood down and waited for breakfast. Fires crackled, and a smell of frying bacon made the post seem better fitted for habitation. A fried egg and three rashers, on a cold enamelled plate, half a loaf of bread and a tin of jam, a brown metal teapot, a tin of milk . . . these became more important than any speculation about the ways of war. They brought with them bodily warmth and a sudden loss of the fatigue of the night, the power to talk naturally and without effort, and the good taste of a pipe of tobacco. Two days and nights followed, uneventful and uncomfortable, with a drizzle of rain to accentuate the feeling that war was mostly a matter of being wet, of struggling for a temporary mastery over mud. Late on the third night we were relieved by another garrison and we marched back stiffly to the ruined houses from which we had set out, years older in body and mind. Down the communication trench, along the Rue Tilleloy, and into the bare kitchen of an abandoned cottage, we walked in a crescendo of appreciation, caring less and less about the fortunes of the sector with every step that increased the distance between us and that servitude of mud. Three days ago this cottage was a poor place, low down in the scale of human habitation, but to-night it promised a glorious ease—so had we changed in this short time. To stand upright before a fire after stooping night and day in a cold dug-out, to walk about on a dry stone floor, to wear dry clothes with no down-dragging weight on the shoulders, to read a paper by candlelight with outstretched legs, to smoke a last pipe by the dying embers; all these, and many other ordinary things, became a high privilege and matter for thanksgiving. The long day ended in a lying down in a warm sleeping bag, on soft straw, and a sudden dropping into a heavy sleep. Our guns were firing, shaking the cottage as they did three nights ago, but their noise was now a thing of no significance —they were our own guns.

I woke up on the morning of Christmas Eve chilled to the bone and very stiff. As I turned over from one side to the other and tucked the upper blanket of my sleeping bag into my shoulder, I noticed that it was damp. A few seconds later I found that the whole of my sleeping bag was wet, the straw sodden, and that there were two inches of water on the floor. I reached for my boots and stepped out of my bag to find that the clothes in which I had slept were wet: a good beginning to this last day of rest. A few nights ago I had gazed at the stars through that hole in the roof, but now I wished that I had repaired it. Little wonder that I was cold and stiff. Had this happened two years earlier I would have waited for pneumonia, but all I did was to change my underclothing and allow the rest to dry upon me.

Another day of inactivity faded into a dull evening, and shortly after dusk we paraded on the road. We were to go to the front line, there to spend our Christmas. Last year there had been much fraternizing with the enemy, but this year strict orders had been issued that we must confine our goodwill not only to our fellow Christians, but to Christians of allied nationality. We were to remain throughout possessed by the spirit of hate, answering any advances with lead. This was the substance of the message read out to us on parade on Christmas Eve; it created no stir, nor did it seem in any way unreasonable at the time. Not one of us, standing on that road, had any desire to show cordiality to an enemy unseen and unknown, whose presence was manifested only in sudden moments of a great uprising of fear. Why should we cherish any thought of sharing with this impersonal cause of our degradation even one arbitrary day of peace? I do not say that we marched up the Rue Tilleloy inspired with a fresh determination to kill at every opportunity on Christmas Day, nor that we meditated a secret overthrowing of the orders that we had received. We reached the front line in a neutral mood, hoping rather for a quiet and uneventful spell of trench duty.

The night was fine and starry, with little wind. The front line trench was wet and poor, flimsier even than Fort Erith—technically speaking it was a breastwork, not a trench. If Fort Erith seemed unfinished, this could not be rated higher than half-begun, with its evil-smelling wet walls, undrained sump-pits and ramshackle dug-outs. There were five officers to share the watch, and when the company commander allotted to me a two-hour period, from one in the morning till three, I felt proud to command a stretch of the front line on my first visit. At dinner that evening a bottle of champagne gave a spurious glow to an ordinary meal, if a first meal in the front line can ever be called ordinary. Towards midnight we heard voices from the German trenches and some snatches of song: they were making merry. The night was still, and its quiet was unbroken by rifle or machine-gun fire. The artillery on both sides sent over a few shells towards the rear of the lines. The firing could rightly be described as desultory, for there was little desire on either side to create trouble; some rounds must of course be fired, otherwise questions would follow.

The battalion on our right was shouting to

the enemy, and he was responding. Gradually the shouts became more deliberate, and we could hear 'Merry Christmas Tommy' and 'Merry Christmas Fritz'. As soon as it became light, we saw hands and bottles being waved at us, with encouraging shouts that we could neither understand nor misunderstand. A drunken German stumbled over his parapet and advanced through the barbed wire, followed by several others, and in a few moments there was a rush of men from both sides, carrying tins of meat, biscuits, and other odd commodities for barter. This was the first time I had seen No Man's Land, and it was now Every Man's Land, or nearly so. Some of our men would not go, and they gave terse and bitter reasons for their refusal. The officers called our men back to the line, and in a few minutes No Man's Land was once more empty and desolate. There had been a feverish exchange of 'souvenirs', a suggestion for peace all day and a football match in the afternoon, and a promise of no rifle fire at night. All this came to naught. An irate Brigadier came spluttering up to the line, thundering hard, throwing a 'court martial' into every other sentence, ordering an extra dose of militant action that night, and breathing fury everywhere. We had evidently jeopardized the safety of the Allied cause. I suspect that across No Man's Land a similar scene was being played, for later in the day the guns became active. The artillery was stimulating the infantry to resume the war. Despite the fulminations of the Generals, the infantry was in no mood for offensive measures, and it was obvious that, on both sides, rifles and machine guns were aimed high.

A few days later we read in the papers that on Christmas Day, 1915, there was no fraternizing with the enemy—hate was too bitter to permit of such a yielding. Our men were wary enough to press as close as they might to the German wire in the hope of concealing from sight the weakness of our own defence. I could find no residue of tenderness towards the enemy as a result of this encounter, nor can I think now that any harm was done. The infantry hated the enemy artillery, and extended an impersonal hate to the opposing infantry if it interfered with the routine of trench life, but the infantry of one side never saw its opponents under the conditions of our soldiering except at times of battle or raiding. What was there of an enemy in an unarmed man clad in a different uniform, eager to secure something of ours in return for some little possession of his own? Let that man be armed, and intent to kill—all would be different, and lead and iron the only commodities for barter.

Turning into the dug-out in the late afternoon, I saw the company commander seated in the corner reading a book, to all appearances far away in another country. At my entry he looked up, and went on reading. Some minutes later I spoke to him as he put down his book.

'You are the first man I have seen in France reading poetry,' said I. He grunted a query.

'Do you read much of it?' I went on to ask.

'Yes . . . do you?'

'I do, whenever I get an opportunity.'

'Now that is where you make a mistake,' he said; 'I make a point of learning by heart one poem a day, no matter where I am. It is the only way to keep sane. What are you reading?'

'I am trying to learn Browning's "Abt Vogler",' I replied.

'Too long,' said he, 'try sonnets. I am learning one of Wordsworth's sonnets each day. . . . Well, I must go out to see what sort of a mess they are making of that new bomb store.'

I attempted later to renew our discussion of poetry, but I met with no success. He retired behind his customary cloud of reserve, speaking only of the numerous practical details of everyday life and sharing with me, in his quiet generous way, his long experience of trench management. I do not know what became of him, but I hope he lived to read his sonnets in better days.

On Boxing Night we were relieved by the Irish Guards. I have no experience of their military virtues, but they greatly enriched my life and enlarged my vocabulary; their oaths and curses were romantic imaginings after the banalities and repetitions of our English swearing, their voices a splash of colour against the grey mud. Back again to the same cottage, but this time by ourselves, for we had finished our apprenticeship. The Guards marched further West, into divisional reserve and rest, and as we said good-bye to them, they were kind enough to praise our discipline. We had approached the Guards a few days ago with some awe, but we left them now with a deep respect for their strong and sturdy self-reliance, and with some understanding of their pride in their regiment.

Green, my servant, was a devoted and untiring worker, and had, I believe, shown his worth as a successful manager of one of the multiple grocery shops in Cricklewood, but he was a poor cook. We sat down to a dinner of fried steak and mashed potatoes, washed down with rum and water, and all night I was very sick. I blamed Green, but it is possible that the water I drank in the line had delayed its ruthless action until that evening.

The next day we went away in buses to a little hamlet called Le Sart, near the Forêt de Nieppe; here the battalion came together again, to talk of great doings in the trenches, and to enjoy the luxury of good billets.

II

COMMAND

COMMAND

We marched through Merville, Vieille Chapelle and Lacouture to Richebourg St. Vaast, an empty shell of a village. Bombardment had driven away all its inhabitants and had left gaping holes in its red-bricked outline. The church was little more than a grey scree of stone, and as the buildings near to it had suffered more severely than those in the outskirts of the village, there was a progression of decayed brickwork visible to the eye. One wall had already become a heap of rubble tidily piled at a street corner so as to allow free movement over the cobbles; a little further back, what was once a house was now but a ten-foot ruin; behind this the curve rose to a house damaged but not disarticulated, with a part of the roof miraculously poised over its frame. Here and there a garden had run wild into long dark grass, and through an orchard on one side ran an aimless trench, now overgrown with weeds. We dumped our equipment in good corners of the most habitable rooms, staking a hasty claim, then finding a better pitch and abandoning the first found, but a burst of shell-fire brought our explorings to a quick end. The enemy had in all probability observed our march, or our entry into the village, and for an hour we were heavily shelled. A shell-burst, even in the soft mud of the trenches, seemed the greatest noise on earth, but when I heard a succession of 'five-nines' hitting these houses I plumbed depths of terror hitherto undiscovered by me. I found it hard to maintain an appearance of unconcern while these monsters were stealing out of the silence into a hiss and a burst, reverberating in a rumble that lingered for some time as if it were loath to cease its echoing. I had begun to eat, but food dried in my mouth. I stopped and lit a cigarette, walked up and down the room, wondering whether it were better to remain indoors, risking a fall of brick, than to be outside, exposed to flying pieces of shell splinters. It did not seem to matter. A greater need was to find something to do, so I went from house to house talking to the small groups of men. In time of danger, the greatest burden of all is enforced inactivity. An hour passed incredibly slowly before the shelling ceased, and when we came to count the cost, we found that two men had been killed, and five seriously wounded.

At night we carried stores up to Richebourg l'Avoué, and there, a little behind the front line, we spent five hours digging a communication trench through the village cemetery—an evil task, even in winter. The next day we were so heavily shelled in our village that we were forced to seek shelter in the scattered trenches and in the ditches outside. That night we went into the front line at Richebourg l'Avoué, to take complete charge of a sector for the first time; the war was now surging round our feet, and it was hard to believe that less than a month ago we were wondering what a trench looked like. This trench was wet and ill-built; there were but few fire-bays where the water was not ankle-deep above the duckboards, and in most parts it was knee-deep. On the extreme right of the company front the trench abandoned its useless struggle against the encroaching water and stopped abruptly, leaving rows of rusty barbed wire entanglements to keep a silent watch on the enemy. At night we sent out a patrol to make contact with our neighbours across the gap. The division we had relieved left its artillery to cover our front—noisy fellows, easily stirred to strife, and much given to wire-cutting. There was water in our narrow dug-out, so narrow that I could not lie full length on the bench at the back of it. It was difficult to sleep, and the labour of wading through water added greatly to the fatigue of the four long days and nights. Our artillery bombarded the enemy's wire, his artillery shelled our trenches in retaliation: our guns, regarding this as an insult, doubled their fury, and the enemy responded to the challenge. The infantry sat and suffered, cursing all artillery, allied or enemy. What task was more pressing than the draining of wet trenches, rebuilding fire-bays, and making dug-outs sound enough to keep out the rain? A dug-out in this sector was not a hole in the ground; it was a child's clumsy effort to build a little one-roomed house, with sandbags full of viscous mud for bricks. It had no foundation, no frame, no structure. For a roof, some sheets of corrugated iron were laid on two or three timbers resting on the sandbag walls, and on the iron a course or two of sandbags. Most of the dug-outs were bullet-proof, certainly, but a direct hit with a light shell would destroy the best of them. If we improved one place, the enemy artillery, responding to our gun-fire, would bring our work to naught. Artillery was meant to cover or to stop an attack; if there was no attack, then let the guns fire at their own true opponents, the enemy artillery. Thus spake the infantry, and I am quite sure that across No Man's Land, Saxon and Bavarian spoke the same words. At this time our guns were short of shells. If we asked the artillery to fire in retaliation for a drubbing of our line, the response did not equal the original offence, which increased our annoyance at what we thought to be wasteful shelling.

At night a trench mortar officer set his guns in a derelict trench about twenty yards behind the line and carried up his ammunition, heavy globes of iron with a little cylindrical projection like a broken handle. In the morning I moved the men from the bays between the trench mortars and their target, to lighten the risk of loss from the retaliatory fire. A pop, and then a black ball went soaring up, spinning round as it went through the air slowly; more pops and more queer birds against the sky. A stutter of terrific detonations seemed to shake the air and the ground, sandbags and bits of timber sailed up slowly and fell in a calm deliberate way. In the silence that followed the explosions, an angry voice called out in English, across No Man's Land, 'YOU BLOODY WELSH MURDERERS.'

The trench mortar team hurried away, pleased with their shooting—as they always were—and left us to wait for the shelling of our line. It did not begin immediately, as we had expected. An hour passed, then another, until the suspense became harder to bear than a bombardment. In the late afternoon, when we had decided that the enemy was going to swallow this insult and we had resumed our mud-building and irrigation, a sudden fury of shell-fire turned our poor trench into a field of spouting volcanoes, spattering mud up into the air. The angry hiss of 77's, the ponderous whirr of 5.9's, the dull empty whack of bombs and the whipping crack of shrapnel all merged into a sea of noise. Ten minutes of this drove us into a stupor of fear, and fear brought its terrible thirst; there was nothing to do but to sit still, half crouched against the wall of the trench, waiting, waiting. Every moment we expected to hear a shout of 'Stretcher-bearers at the double', but it never came. The storm ended as suddenly as it began; now was the time to count the cost. By some uncommon stroke of luck, not one man was wounded or killed, and in ten minutes we drank the best cup of tea ever made on this earth.

We found the cottage marked 'Company

Mess' to be furnished a little better than its counterpart in other villages. There was a good lamp, a marble-topped sideboard, and one arm-chair upholstered in red plush. Madame was willing to lend us plates and cups, provided that we paid for any damage done. Two of our subalterns, stirred by this sudden luxury, had gone to Béthune to buy a gramophone, 'lorry-hopping' there and back. Two records had been broken on the journey home, but two had survived; one a song called 'Red Devon', the other a song whose title was, I think, 'Galway by the Sea'. I have forgotten the words of both, and the tune of the first, but I shall never forget the melody of the second. It was an ordinary ballad, poor enough, and soaked in sentiment, buoyed up by the most conventional of chord sequences, but for me it is one of a few pieces of music that set in motion a whole complex of waves. The waves of sound are the least important in this response; I see more than I hear. A shuttered room, an oil lamp throwing dingy shadows of a bottle of wine and a loaf on a table covered with yellow varnished American cloth; maps and type-written orders, a Sam Browne belt hanging over the back of a chair, Billy sitting down with unbuttoned tunic, brooding silently, his young face clouded and morose, hearing in the simple tune a world of things he could not say; other good men who shared with me the hard days of war but did not live to look back upon them with a profound and unending feeling of miraculous deliverance. Music is a key that can open strange rooms in the house of memory. Some time after this, I rejoined my battalion in a village far behind the line. I was at the very nadir of my military fortunes, having failed, for ever as I thought, to secure a prize so near to my hand. As I walked along the village street to the company mess, I heard a gramophone playing Chaminade's 'Danse Créole', and I can never hear it now without its accompaniment of failure and despondency.

After an evening and a day of listening to these two ballads, we began to wish for some variety of entertainment. The two broken records were in a lighter vein, we were told. A longing for any part of England must needs be set in a minor key of sentiment, but a yearning for the Southern states of America could find a cheerful expression. Another trip to Béthune brought into our repertoire a syncopated ditty with the ironical title of 'This is the Life'. Three lines of it have wedged themselves into my memory, possibly because of their vivid untruth:

I love the cows AND chickens
BUT this is the life,
OH this is the life. . . .

The rest of the song has faded away, buried by that very life of which it sang.

In these days we went more than half-way to meet and welcome any diversion to the eye or the ear, or any colouring of the ever-moving but never-changing environment. It was this that made of a gramophone, and of Kirchner's drawings of thin-legged, silk-stockinged women, not a luxury, nor a decoration, but furniture in every mess. The drawings were pinned on the dingy walls of country cottages whose women-folk seemed of another species, not easily recognizable as contemporary, and in dug-outs where the silk stockings shone against the background of sackcloth. They pleased the eye, but a cynic might say that they offered nothing more than a liqueur to a man parched with thirst.

The company commander was reading the battalion orders, beginning with the duties of the morrow, passing through the local gossip and the much-travelled snippets of wisdom from G.H.Q., when he burst into laughter. The mess was lingering over a bottle of thin red wine of unknown derivation, and we looked up in surprise.

'Griff,' he said, 'you have got a job.'

'What is it?' I asked.

'Listen. . . . A Brigade class in cookery will be held at Battalion Headquarters—why, it's to-morrow—one company cook will be detailed from each battalion to report at ten a.m.—you've got to take command of the class.'

'I command a cookery class? Why, it's nonsense—what do I know about cooking? I'm going to see the adjutant now. . . . Hand me my belt.'

I disappeared, leaving behind me a cackle of laughter and much wit about the sick parades that would follow, and found the adjutant finishing his coffee. I harangued him and argued with him, but to no purpose; it was a Brigade order, and the order said that I was to take command of the class. The only advice I could get was to stay up all night trying to rake together some semblance of knowledge, but I did convince him that the assistance of the battalion master-cook was essential to the success of the venture.

I traced the expert to an outhouse where he stood knife in hand, a grimy figure, flanked by enormous sides of bacon, pieces of cheese, and sacks full of bread.

'Sergeant, you've got to start a cooking class with me to-morrow morning.'

'Yes, sir,' he said calmly, as if this were a matter of no moment.

'You had better begin thinking hard what to do and say, for I'm blest if I know anything about cooking. You'll have to do the talking. The class is going to last for four solid days. How on earth are we to keep these fellows quiet for all that time?'

'Don't you worry, sir—we'll find 'em plenty to do . . . I got'n idea, sir . . . I was on a class myself once. . . . We'll teach them to make ovens and to make puddings.'

'Splendid,' said I; 'I like the "We".'

'Don't you fret, sir, I'll come round at nine o'clock to-morrow and we'll find a good place for to teach 'em.'

I walked back to the mess and burrowed in the depths of my kit-bag until I found that encyclopædia of military lore—Field Service Regulations. There was sure to be something about cooking in this manual—indeed I had a dim recollection of drawings of ovens and neatly arranged pots and dixies. I sat up late that night, fuddling my brain with technical terms until I felt confident of my ability to conceal my ignorance behind vague sentences full of the jargon of the craft. I had served long enough in the army to know the value of words. To throw a few 'bracketings' into a talk with a gunner, or to introduce an odd 'revetment' into a conversation with an engineer, was more than a friendly acknowledgement of the importance of his trade in your everyday life; it created an atmosphere of temporary equality, of unity of purpose, and a presupposition of vast reserves of undisclosed knowledge. Being infantry, we had no rich vocabulary of craft jargon, and we succumbed easily to the temptation to use other people's words, with a slight self-consciousness in their handling.

In the morning Sergeant Smith came to my billet, looking strangely clean and fresh, so different from the stew-coloured figure of the evening that I stared at him.

'Put my best tunic on, sir, and I washed my overalls last night and put them in the cook-house to dry.' In his hand he held an unused note-book, a badge of his new office. We walked to a farmhouse where he had discovered a small unused barn, open on one side, with a wooden table: this was to be our laboratory.

'If you was to go to the Quartermaster-Sergeant, sir, and ask him to save some currants and a bit of flour, I could show them how to make a pudding. He'd do it for you, sir, he would, and I could get a few things together here ready to start.'

I went obediently, and was promised currants, but there was no flour.

'No matter, sir, we'll show 'em how to make flour from biscuits.'

Four men arrived, dumped their rifles and kit in a corner, and stood in a row while I addressed them.

'The object of this course', said I, with an air of great wisdom, 'is to see what can be done to vary the diet, using only the rations that are issued. We think it possible to make boiled puddings, to roast meat, and to make rissoles with bully and biscuit.' Sergeant Smith nodded encouragingly. 'I'm sure you'll agree that it is worth going to a little trouble to get a change from stew and curried stew. Sergeant Smith will give demonstrations. Carry on, Sergeant.'

He carried on. He pounded biscuits into flour, made a currant pudding, using bacon drip for lard, tied the agglomerate in a new sandbag, and boiled it in a dixie. I went for a walk while the pudding boiled, and came back to find five men eating it. I joined them. It was a plain unobjectionable pudding of the plum duff variety, very filling, but undoubtedly a pudding. The sandbag left a certain amount of fluff, but not enough to worry a soldier. Encouraged by this success, we made rissoles of bully, powdered biscuit and bacon drip—they were also very satisfying. Our greatest triumph was the conversion of two oil drums into an oven—I call this 'our' triumph because my ignorance of cooking did not prevent me from giving assistance in the solution of a mechanical problem. The ordinary field oven of the text-book was a hit and miss affair; you put a fire in your oven, raked it out and put the meat in, and when you took out the joint it was cooked—or not. Using two oil drums, we contrived to maintain a fire under the oven while the joint was being cooked, and we were able to open the oven to turn the meat.

One afternoon the Brigadier called to see us. He said he would sample our cooking, so we offered him a rissole and a slab of currant duff. He praised them highly, and bravely ate both. He already had the Victoria Cross. The class was a success, and he said that it was to be repeated on every occasion of our coming out of the line, and that I was to take charge of it. I walked with him towards the road.

'Do you inspect the men's rifles every morning?' he asked.

'Yes, sir,' said I, vowing to start the next morning.

'Where did you pick up your knowledge of cooking?'

'I haven't any, sir; all the cooking I have ever done is to make my own breakfast in Chambers in the Temple.'

'Well, you've got a good sergeant, which is equally to your credit.'

I taught nothing, but I learnt a great deal. When we went back to the line I gave permission to the company cooks to stay behind with the cooker on condition that the rations were supplemented every night by a boiled pudding or rissoles; if the supplement were lacking, they were to come up to the line next day. The supply never failed.

In our early days in the line, the multitude of small cares and the unbroken sequence of starting a score of new tasks in different places, all calling for constant supervision, brought with them a strange busyness. The body moved from bay to bay, tiring itself in the long hours of wading through mud and water. Four days in the trenches were four days and nights of walking and standing, with shoulders aching from the drag of wet clothes. To lie down for two hours on a plank, half sinking into a dream-ridden sleep, half hearing every noise within the radius of audibility, imagining in every step that approached the dug-out a summons to return to the world of concentrated attention; this was little rest to body or to mind. On such a bed flesh was no protection to the bones; it was a small envelope containing a jumble of crossing nerves, warring with themselves, and raised to a state of red-hot sensitivity. Bone pressed down upon, and wood forced up against this thin cushion until the sting changed slowly into a dragging pain. Getting up was a process of re-assembling the members; arms were stiff, though near at hand, legs had travelled further from control, but feet were far away in a cold and distant land. A queer lightness in the knees enhanced the weight of the feet, making the leg a lever too fragile to bear such a load at its extremity. A waking man was a slack-stringed fiddle, to be tuned up peg by peg into the full tension of self-command.

There was always something to be done, involving a movement and a standing about. Digging, filling sandbags, building, carrying stores and ammunition, repairing the walls damaged by shell fire, scheming against the insidious attack of water, strengthening the barbed wire, resetting duckboards; an officer did none of these things with his own hands, or but rarely. He was there when such things were done, and being there demanded a presence of body and of mind. These tasks, in our early days, seemed to be of such importance that their supervision became an occupation capable of absorbing one's entire stock of energy. They filled the mind so fully that a bombardment became a troublesome interruption of the serious business of life in the trenches.

Later, however, the redistribution of mud took the second place, for the men knew what to do; the zeal of the beginner faded into the semi-drudgery of the journeyman. Days and nights passed by in an oscillation between a suddenly roused fear of instant death and a slowly increasing dread of the continuance of this life of atrophy. An enemy we never saw—no, not an enemy, for maiming or extinction came from a bursting of iron in a ditch, the result of a mathematical computation made some miles away, tragically wrong to us, while the arithmetician knew not whether his answer were right.

Across No Man's Land there were men

sharing trouble with us, fighting the same losing battle against water, powerless before the sudden storm of bursting metal, and longing to be home again with their children. Were they an enemy? A scrap of song floating across at dusk, or a grey helmet seen for a moment through a periscope—were we to freeze into hatred at these manifestations of a life so like our own? An unrelieved weariness drugged us into a dullness of mind so overpowering that the brain declined a metaphysical battle on these issues. Everything was unreason, and it profited not to refine the ricidulous into the mad. On the other side of Aubers Ridge a German gunner twirled a few wheels into a new position, moved a bar of iron, and sent death soaring into the air; he went to his dinner. While he was moving his wheels and dials, three Londoners were filling sandbags in a ditch on the plain, arguing about Tottenham Hotspur. A flash, a noise, and a cloud of smoke.

'Blast 'em, they've killed old Parkinson—blown 'is 'ead off, they 'ave, the bastards.'

Blast whom? The unseen German, going to his dinner? The man who sang, over the way? No. Blast everybody and everything; blast all who contributed to the sending of this quiet middle-aged Londoner to die in a ditch, in no combat between men, but in a struggle between two sets of mathematical equations. Did we think out this bitter problem, or discuss the ways of bringing an end to this distemper? No . . . we were too tired. Blast them, and back to the weary lifting of mud, this time passing a stretcher covered with a blanket hiding all but a thin trickle of blood. Four children, and his wife's name was 'Liz' . . . must write to her to-night. . . . Oh, blast them!

While the mind was spinning slowly round a pivot of 'How long?' the muscles were carrying an aching frame back and fro along a wet and sour-smelling trench, finding each journey more difficult than the one before. How long must we wait for the relief? How long could one hope to live, after two months of daily escape? How long would it be before we could get leave? How long could this war last? This was the series of concentric circles of sentences passing through a deadened mind, each one repeated again and again, a new way of 'counting sheep', dulling the brain into a half-sleep. Four days in the line can be written down as a rapid fall along the slope of vitality into a stupor of weariness; on the path, some sharp crests of fear, but the end was overwhelming fatigue. Now that the war is half-forgotten, many men have described trench life, some with a wealth of remembered detail both of doing and of saying, rebuilding for the reader a day, a place and a people. Some clever writers have found in an early morning visit to the line material enough to furnish a vivid background for a long play of wit and character. But to most of us who served in the infantry, the thought of a trench brings back that long span of damnable tiredness, broken here and there by a sudden dry-tongued spasm of fear. Cold nights, the discomfort of wet clothes, dragging minutes of anxiety on patrol, the sufferings of men . . . these are all fading with the passing years, but nothing can efface the memory of that all-conquering fatigue.

The days were lengthening and February had filled the dykes to overflowing. There was a theory that the Germans, with the cunning of which they were the sole proprietors, had contrived to drain all the water from their trenches into ours. The men were convinced of its truth. It was easy enough to believe that Germany made no mistakes in any matter calling for the exercise of long-ranged scientific knowledge, and also to credit the enemy with a complete mastery over the material conditions of war. Wherever we had stood in a trench, the Germans were above us, looking down from some ridge upon our amateurish struggles on the plain. We had not seen the enemy's trenches except through a periscope or a sniper's peep-hole, but among the men it was accepted as inevitable that these trenches should be dry, and full of safe and comfortable dug-out. We lived in a world of our own mistakes, compelled by the unsuccess of our commanders, as we thought, to inhabit a sodden and water-logged plain, failing to make a dry trench or a comfortable dug-out. We knew the crashing terrors of the enemy's 'five-nines', and the malignant punch of his 'seven-sevens', but we had not as yet been shelled by our own artillery, so we could not believe that our shell-fire equalled his in malevolence. Our guns might have been excellent weapons, but we were short of shells, and, one afternoon, a call for retaliation on the enemy's trenches brought seventeen rounds of 4.5's, of which fourteen failed to explode. For our comforting we were told that there was an unlimited supply of ammunition to fire if the enemy attacked us; if his infantry left their trenches to advance, our S.O.S. barrage would be impenetrable. Our day-to-day firing, however, was severely restricted. Standing up to the knees in water, half ashamed of the weakness of our gunfire, it was easy to convince oneself that on the other side of No Man's Land dwelt a master of the craft of war, planning superhuman schemes for our destruction at the time of his choosing. Not that we thought the grey-hatted infantrymen opposite to be one whit more able than ourselves to kill or to harass; the skill lay further back, in their commanders. Thus it came that hundreds of men believed that the water in our trenches was one of Germany's many weapons, and when one of our engineers strongly denied this possibility, his listeners saw in this denial another demonstration of our inferiority—in intelligence.

This great question of drainage remained unsettled when we left this sector, moving south towards the La Bassée canal to take charge of a marsh in front of Festubert. On our right the ground ran up to Givenchy, an ill-famed hillock where the pulse of war quickened to a restless exchange of shell-fire and bombs. We were quiet enough in Festubert. Water had triumphed over man, and there was no front line to hold. The greater part of the battalion lived in a well-made breastwork some hundreds of yards away from the enemy, but my company held the Islands, a series of isolated posts in the marsh. Small groups of men spent the day lying down quietly in a short stretch of trench, with nothing whatever to do but to look through a periscope. There were no communication trenches leading up to these posts, and by day they were unapproachable from the rear or from their neighbours. There were frequent reliefs of the garrisons from the main body of the company, scattered about in bricked-up dug-outs made out of the ruins of the village. Visiting these posts at night was an eerie business, walking boldly above ground, across ditches and through the remains of barbed wire, past long-unburied corpses, up to the island posts. The wire in front was bad, and the loss of direction on a dark night carried a risk of stumbling into the German lines. A hard frost set in, and a heavy fall of snow added greatly to our troubles, making life a mere struggle to keep warm. At night we lit fires in braziers, but by day the smoke would draw shell-fire upon our dug-outs, so we had to school ourselves to bear the ache of cold in inactivity, discovering in the process several new forms of stiffness. Our numbers were declining steadily with each visit to the line. On parade the company had shrunk to one half its original size, although we could not recall to memory any one day of large loss; the tree was shedding its leaves in its early autumn, and ever before us was the prospect of the gale of a battle that would strip us bare. The growing pressure of day added to day had made inelastic creatures of us all, incapable of reaction against good fortune or bad, dragging one foot after another upon the slow-moving treadmill of this weary life, torpid minds in unresponsive bodies. There was nothing new to talk about, one day was like another.

At last something happened to rouse us a little. We heard that a platoon of Bantams was coming to us to serve an apprenticeship in the line. Were we already old enough in the ways of war to teach others? It was not difficult to persuade ourselves that we were veterans, for years seemed to have passed by since we 'came out of our time' with the Guards. A whole platoon of fresh men to help us in carrying and in digging was a great reinforcement. The Bantams were small, but very sturdy and self-possessed; on parade they seemed to be all equipment, and on the march, walking bundles of gear. The Londoners gave them a great welcome, and I heard many a traveller's tale being told to the newcomers. This I overheard in a dug-out in Festubert.

'I tell you what, kid, the shells ain't so bad, nor the bullets ain't, nor the blarsted fatigues. It's the bleedin' rats as does it. When you're standin' on guard at night they runs abaht on the parapet and lashes out at yer with their bleedin' 'ind legs and if you ain't careful they knocks yer off the bleedin' fire-step back inter the trench.'

'And it ain't only that,' said another. 'Look what they did to Sergeant Tracy. Now 'e was farst asleep in a dug-out, 'e was, and when 'e woke up, blowed if a rat 'adn't bitten off 'alf 'is blinkin' ear.'

' 'Ave yer seen the Cap'n's mackintosh?' asked a third. 'Just you look at the collar when 'e comes round to-night. You'll find one 'alf of it all gone, all chewed away by a rat when 'e was sleepin'. Big fat things they are, big as dogs, and fat as 'ell.'

The very first night the Bantams accompanied us to the line, the Germans opposite called out 'Cock-a-doodle-do' many times. There was no mistaking it: they knew perfectly well that the Bantams were with us. We on our part, in the infantry, did not know whether a Bavarian or a Saxon stood against us, so that this display of knowledge brought to us all an uneasy feeling that every movement we made was put down in some enormous note-book on the other side. Here was clear proof that the German High Command was omniscient, and there was a large increase in the supporters of the theory that their infinite cunning enabled the Germans to drain all their water into our trenches.

Four days of this hard weather were a severe trial of our powers of resistance. Hands and feet were sore when we set out on our trudge along the road to Gorre, the pack seemed heavier than usual, and the rifle made of lead. We started stiffly in small parties at five minute intervals, the Sergeant-Major and I walking at the rear of the last section. Traffic had turned the snow into slush, and men were staggering uneasily on the slippery road, sometimes falling into the drifts at the side, everybody silent, tired and sleepy. On along this never-ending lane, following a dark ribbon of trodden snow, bearing occasionally into the ditch to let pass by a limber waggon taking up supplies, regaining the crown of the road with increasing difficulty, and halting awhile to rest. At every halt it grew harder to restart this toiling train of men. The Bantams were suffering severely, for their feet were not inured to the soaking, and their packs, equipment and rifles weighed nearly as much as themselves. The Sergeant-Major and I ended by driving these weary men like sheep, with curses and pushes, carrying several rifles, dragging back on to his feet every man who dropped down, allowing no one, upon any pretext, to rest. Cruel work, but kinder than letting men of low vitality drop into an endless sleep. Three hours after the first section of the company reached Gorre we brought in this tail of stupefied stragglers, pushed them into a barn and gave them a tot of rum; they were half asleep as they took off their equipment and dropped into the straw. I drank half a cupful of rum and began to nibble at a biscuit, but I was too sleepy to finish it.

III

GIVENCHY

GIVENCHY

GIVENCHY had a bad reputation. There were parts of the line that seemed to possess some quality of bitter enmity, seemed rather to be possessed by some demon of unrest, as if a battle once begun there had never ended. Each one stood, in the minds of all who knew it, as a focus of evil—a hearth whereon the fire of hatred had never died down to the ashes of a perfunctory showing of the daily discourtesies of war. War, like other diseases, has its routine: the exchange of artillery-fire and rifle-fire at stand-to in the cold of dawn, followed by an interval of tranquillity while both sides broke their fast, then a definite programme of wire-cutting or trench bombardment by the artillery, fading into a slackening of gun-fire during the night lest the flashes should disclose the positions of the guns. In the dark, both sides mended their broken wire and patrolled No Man's Land. This one might describe, not inaccurately, as the daily routine of trench warfare, and, like all routine in man's life, it was subject to cataclysmic upheaval from time to time, when orders came to the infantry to carry out a raid of the enemy's lines.

Nevertheless, there was a feeling that these disturbances were a passing fever, and that the routine would triumph over all. This conviction —for it was strong enough to warrant the name— would manifest itself in a personal resentment against the assumed authors of this torment, invariably personified as some unknown pundits far removed from its dangers. We were in a state of war, admittedly, but the admission had to fight hard against an inborn desire for peace at the moment. At the time, and for long after, no opportunity was lost of impressing upon the minds and hearts of all that it was by means of such 'demonstrations' (as they were called) that the 'ascendency' over the enemy was gained. We were doubtful, sceptical even, at the time, for the balance of profit was not to be measured by our eyes. Twelve years have now gone by, and each year is strengthening the conviction that there was wisdom in the instinct of the humble soldier; I do not think that the theory of attrition has many adherents now, at any rate, not among those who served in the infantry. There was, in fact, a profound difference between sectors where routine triumphed and those whose quality took the form of a permanent manifestation of evil.

The fire of bitter antagonism never died down to ashes in such places as Givenchy: the wind of every passing shell would fan the embers into a blaze of fury. Battle strode the air like a demon, and cast its shadow over this accursed hill, night and day, without respite; pillars of fire and clouds of smoke were here no signs of wonder. What I have called the routine of war may be likened to the mood of a man sullen in temper, but here man was in a rage. One could not believe that the mechanical processes of war determined the whole of this quality, that peace would brood over Givenchy as soon as the noise of the guns subsided. No such metamorphosis was credible, so strong was the feeling of the presence of malignant fate hovering above this hillock in a plain. It seemed rather as if nothing that man could do would ever succeed in bringing quiet to this village.

The eye could catch no promise in the landscape. In many places Spring broke out into a riot of green hedges and blossoming orchards, a little further North one could look backwards from the line, over a small desert of destruction, into an abandoned garden struggling into life at the bidding of April. A small thing perhaps, but enough to stand for sanity to a mind obsessed with the greyness of the mud underfoot. Givenchy could not yield even this grain of comfort. Broken crucifixes, shattered walls, unmended roads, and splintered tree trunks—it was typical of war as waged in our day. There was ugliness everywhere one looked, the ugliness of smashed new brick and new plaster, a terrible ugliness, inconceivable to one who has seen no ruins but those of aged walls, mellowed by sun, wind and rain.

Why does a new thing broken look so much older than a ruin of the Middle Ages? When the setting sun strikes the towers of Harlech Castle, it is easy to forget that cruel things have happened in its dark dungeons: it is indeed hard to believe fully that this house on the rock was ever a frame for the daily adventure of man and woman. It is difficult to imagine that the grey walls were linked with the life of man: in their long rest they have acquired another dignity, derived not from association with humanity, but rather from centuries of withdrawal from this contact. They dwell apart in a permanent retreat, they wear the sun in splendour and the mists with dignity. In the jagged outline and the broken walls of an old castle, the eye of the beholder sees only the fatigue of long years, and the simple, manly way in which such a noble creature grows old.

So have I seen many an old farmhouse, shelled into a formless jumble of brick, stone and tile, still retain a dignity of demeanour, as if it quietly insisted on recognition. 'Wars come and go,' it seemed to say, 'and men with them, but land must be tilled, and men will be wiser soon; when they have shed their distemper in an orgy of breaking life and limb they will come back to me in penitence.' Man made these old brown dwellings, and they in their turn made men—man unmade them, but in the days to come they will once again make men. They gave shelter to many generations of peasants who toiled to fill the sharp-roofed barns with food, they shook to the tramp of Spanish, French and British soldiers in the old forgotten wars, and suffered at the hands of many nations, but they were not long deflected from their stubborn purpose. An inherent nobility that never left them, even in their present hour of trial, gave to these broken walls an element of strength—it was as if they were looking forward into time, waiting to be restored to their proper usage when man had wearied of his rage.

But I have never seen a new house broken that did not chill the heart of the beholder with its air of unyielding futility. Some, with their ragged profiles, enlarged and gaping window-holes, looked like the faces of gibbering idiots, mad and meaningless, not in any way tragic. When the sun shone full on these red masks they seemed to be laughing emptily, like a maniac who has no fear of evil. They could not stand silent, like a broken church, in a mute protest against the folly of war; they screeched their defiance of man's mastery over their poor and tenuous bodies. And yet it was but a few years since they throbbed to the pulsing life within them. They were not built to store the yield of the fertile soil around, so that one generation should nourish another: they were brought into being to serve the present. But who can look at the shell of a new house where, a little while ago, man and woman began an era of joy in marriage, little children ran about and played, where happiness prevailed over every other mood—who can look at this newly-broken toy, even on a sunny day in early summer, with eyes that can for one moment forget the bitter folly that caused its breaking? The battered frame of the Cloth Hall at Ypres never lost an air of grandeur, but the ruins of Givenchy village looked paltry, in spite of the many lives that were spilt to hold it as ours.

There was a curse on Givenchy village, a curse of blood and a curse of water. A mile to the north stood Festubert, where man fought more with water than with his fellow men; a mile or two to the south the trenches were dry, but on Givenchy hill there was no respite from fire or flood, nor from that devil's volcano of a sprung mine. To stand in the trench was to wait to be blown up, without warning, from below, or to be struck down by some terror from the sky in the shape of a bomb, grenade or shell. We were spared the danger of bullets by the configuration of the ground while we were on the hill, but the approaches to it were swept with machine-gun fire, especially at night when reliefs and fatigue parties were moving. The feeling of waiting, waiting for sudden death all but overpowered a man, to be but half forgotten when he ate or talked. In a sector where there is no mining, an absence of shell fire brings rest to the mind for a while, until one begins to wonder when the shelling will start afresh, but mining puts an end to all repose.

More than a month passed in this slavery, and we were tethered to this hill by a rope that never stretched far enough to allow us to forget its existence. One afternoon in early April I was standing in a trench on the hill, looking westwards over the parados towards Béthune and watching an enormous flock of starlings swaying back and fro in their peculiar mass formation. They were some miles away, black against a glowing sky, so like a half-deflated airship blown about by a gentle breeze that I did not laugh when a sentry asked me if that was a Zeppelin. I handed him my glasses, and believed him when he said that he 'Ain't never seed anythink like that before'. I walked down the trench towards the company dug-out, the first dug-out we had ever dwelt in, for all the other shelters on the marshland were built up, not dug out. Tea was ready, and as we sat down to eat, a runner came stumbling down the wet steps with a message for me from Battalion Headquarters.

'You are detailed to attend a four days' conference at Aire beginning at 10.00 hours on April 10th on Co-operation between artillery and infantry. You will proceed to the cross-roads in A 24 b where a bus will meet you at 18.30 hours to-day April 9th. . . . Acknowledge.'

'Green!' I shouted.

'Coming, sir.'

'Get my kit together, all that I have with me here, and go down to the horse lines and get the rest of it. We've got to be at the cross-roads outside Gorre at half-past six to catch a bus—mind you get the stuff there in good time. You are coming with me.' A clatter of enamelled plates and a 'So long, mate' showed that Green was off.

This was good news, for Aire was a pleasant town. Four days in good billets, dining in a hotel, shop windows to look at—no mud, no shells, no mines. As I left the dug-out it began to rain, but it did not seem to matter much; nothing mattered, for I was going away from these damnable trenches. I did not take any intellectual interest in co-operation between artillery and infantry—the artillery never satisfied the infantry, though at Givenchy it was admitted, grudgingly, that they shot well, considering. Considering what, I do not know, unless it be considering that they were not infantry! However, Aire was Aire, and the learned might talk as they liked.

There was no time to change my uniform or my underclothing, so I joined Green at the cross-roads to wait for the bus. It was dark when we reached Aire. My orders were to go to the Town Major's Office and to ask him for a billet. I entered his clerk's room cold and stiff, wet to the skin, unshaved and incredibly dirty, my clothes caked with mud.

As I was talking to his clerk, the Town Major, a bright-eyed and fresh-looking man of about sixty-five, evidently a retired officer, came out of his room.

'What is it you want?' said he, in a kindly tone of voice, casting his glance over my servant and me, and then turning towards my kit and his rifle.

'I have been told to report to you for a billet, sir,' I replied. 'I am attending a course in Co-operation. . . .'

'Oh yes, I know all about that. What's your name?'

I told him.

'Where have you come from?'

'From Givenchy, sir. . . . I'm sorry I'm in such a mess, but I had to come straight down here from the line, and I have had no time to change.'

'Givenchy . . . a bad place, especially in this weather.' He turned to his clerk and said:

'Send this officer to Number 11 in the Rue . . . (I have forgotten its name) . . . that's a good billet, isn't it?'

'Yes, sir, but Colonel Brown is going there,' said his clerk.

'Colonel Brown can go somewhere else—this gentleman has come straight from the trenches, and the infantry get the best billets in my town,' replied the Town Major.

To many people this will seem so obviously what ought to have happened that to call it a kind action would be an unnecessary underlining of one event in the daily routine of a Town Major's life, barely distinguishable from its neighbour in time. But the practice of war is the pursuit of a straight road, the search for an even way of mechanical progress that avoids a descent into cruelty as carefully as it forbears to rise into kindness; the aim is rather to decline battle with the feelings by confining thought to the impersonal aspect of every situation. It is so much easier at the moment to deal with units than to acknowledge the man inside the uniform. No word came oftener to the lips than 'men', as one would say, 'Send three men to Sap B, and tell them to hold it at all cost. They must throw two bombs for every one that comes over.' A 'man', in this usage, was no more than the temporary overseer of a weapon of destruction, the indispensable, but imperfect, servant of a potential gas asleep in a powder. Man, to a Town Major, was the envelope of a ration of food, the tenant of a bed. In this way, and in no other, lay sanity, for no man could escape madness who turned the impersonal and dessicated 'man' into a living creature with body to kill and soul to hurt. So it came that when the formula broke down, and an elderly man living in comfort in Aire saw before him a youth bearing on his body the outward marks of hardship and discomfort, and in his eye that dullness brought by danger and strain and lack of sleep, a mute and unformed protest took refuge in a kindly deed, long forgotten by the doer, but remembered by me to this distant day.

It was dark, and still raining, when I walked across the Grande Place, pursued by a memory of an earlier visit to this little town. So much had passed, so many events had stubbornly refused to pass, indenting for themselves a permanent depression in the roundness of the mind, that when my servant asked me if I had ever been to Aire before this visit, I thought that a 'No' would have rung as true as my 'Yes'.

'Yes, Green, I came here once, when we were billeted at Warne, to fetch some cakes for the Colonel's mess. I rode here on the water-cart horse, the first time I saw Aire, and the first time that I rode a horse. . . . No more war for four days, anyway, and by the time we finish here the battalion ought to be out of the trenches and in rest billets, so we might have twelve days of comfort and civilization.'

'Any chance of leave, sir?' said Green.

'None at all, as far as I can see—the married men with children are getting the first whack at the vacancies, so I hear.'

We halted at the door of a well-groomed town house standing obscurely in a cobbled street leading nowhere, and I rang the bell. I explained to Madame that I was billeted with her, and gave her a chit from the Town Major to warrant my presence. Through the open door I could see that the house was well furnished, with a look of polished cleanliness that put me to shame to think that man could be so dirty and tiles so clean. She was a woman of sixty, with a sad, quiet face and a gentle voice, and I felt at once that I must do something to atone for my condition. It was so obvious that her life was a battle against dirt, in which she triumphed, and that I was a loser in a similar conflict. I would not enter until I had scraped off my boots and my waterproof all that could be removed of that grey clinging mud of the Low Country, while she stood waiting in the hall, a still black figure against the dimly lit background.

'There is a room at the back where your servant can place your luggage until you require it,' said Madame, and Green passed through into some remote back-kitchen that I never visited, taking with him our dirty gear.

'Would Monsieur like to see his room? It is all ready, and there is a bathroom.'

'Could I have a bath, Madame?'

'Certainly, if your servant will carry up the hot water.'

'I'll look at my room, but I won't go into it until I have had a bath and changed my clothes.'

As we talked we went upstairs, and I saw a carpeted bedroom, with a four-poster bed, and linen so white that it seemed unreal. A carpet and a bed—the ordinary things of life, one would say, of ordinary life, but not of the life of the infantry officer in France. We were invariably billeted in cottages and farmhouses, where the bedrooms had red-tiled floors and whitewashed walls. I had spent five months in France, but this was the first time I had seen a carpet on the floor, and it was many months before I saw another. I thanked Madame, and in the simple words of a man stating the obvious I said how pleased and how fortunate I was. Had she a bedroom for my servant? Yes, there was a room he could have, so we were both to revel in comfort.

I went to the bathroom and smoked a cigarette while I took off my dirty clothes and piled them in a corner. Half an hour later I was shaved and clean and hungry, and when I came downstairs I was invited to drink a glass of wine with Madame, while we discussed the war, the dearness of food, and the difficulty of getting meat. By this time Givenchy was far away, and I felt a man again; war had receded into a background of unreality, not to be revived until, a little later, on leaving the house to search for an hotel at which to dine, I could see in the sky the flickering glow of gun-flashes away in the East, bringing with it the thought of some poor devils standing in the mud and waiting.

A good dinner—for so it seemed,—a bottle of wine shared with another infantry officer from the Bantam Division whom I had already met in the line, and early to bed. The poet who sang of the 'rough male kiss of blankets' had strayed in his choice of emphasis, I felt, as I turned down the linen sheets and glided into their cool, clean embrace.

The four days that followed were spent in eating and sleeping, rioting in the glory of bearing no responsibility for anybody's actions but my own. Between meals I sat meekly at the back of a long room, where learned Artillery Colonels dwelt upon the possibilities of co-operation between artillery and infantry, while peevish Brigadiers and Colonels of infantry complained of the shortcomings of their own artillery. What artillery ever succeeded in pleasing the infantry? Either the artillery was too active, bringing retaliation upon the infantry, or it was too lethargic, inflicting no hurt upon the enemy infantry. I listened and made a few notes of matters mostly beyond my comprehension, knowing full well that nothing different would happen, however much we talked. My friend from the Bantam Division and I were the only junior officers present, and as was fitting, we kept silence, concealing our ignorance of the possibilities of artillery, and only revealing by an occasional mutual glance what we knew of its actualities.

I discovered the Town Major's name, and remembered that some friends of mine knew him well, so I called upon him and made known this common friendship. He was interested and pleased, and he invited me to dine with him at his mess. I do not remember much about the dinner, save that it was a quiet, gentlemanly and pleasant affair. It seemed to be another link with sanity, free from any fever of war, and free from any attempt to forget war; without aiming at distraction, it succeeded in giving a slight but noticeable deflection to the course of one's mind. I have forgotten what we talked about, but there remains this memory of a quiet precision of happenings from soup to the cheese, a sense of order prevailing in this one room, as if the neatness of the dinner were a symbol of a well ordered life. As a Town Major of a town not occupied by the headquarters of any high formation, he was all but omnipotent. Traces of the old Spanish occupation of the Lowlands were still visible in the buildings that framed the Grande Place, and traces of my host's love of order and his tidiness of mind were now to be seen in the carefully erected signboards, direction posts, and billet numbers; one military occupation superimposed upon another, at an interval of some centuries.

One morning as I was shaving, I scraped my chin too closely for comfort, and after breakfast I went in search of some cream to rub into my skin. There was never any difficulty in buying toilet accessories—not a village but you could buy brilliantine, shaving cream, razor blades, and tinctures of every colour and smell. The British Army must have consumed some thousands of tons of these commodities. I paid a franc or two for a pot of cream—I remember even now that it was a white china pot, that it was made by Roger et Gallet, and that it was called 'Crême Vera Violette'. Why this unimportant detail should remain in memory I cannot guess. I used it once, but it was very highly scented, and it found its way into some corner of my kit-bag. There it stayed for some weeks until, when I was home on leave, my wife found the pot and seized it, counting it a great treasure not to be had in England in those days.

On my last day in Aire I said good-bye to Madame and went to the Town Major's office to discover where my battalion was to be found. It was out of the line, and at a little hamlet called Hingette. I found my way there, looking forward eagerly to finding a batch of letters, for I had had none in Aire, and it seemed a long time since I had heard from Wyn. On a warm and sunny Spring day I reached the hamlet of Hingette, nestling in a spread of green meadows at the foot of a little hill, peaceful, and half hiding behind its poplars and fruit trees. I came to our company mess, in a clean and bare red-tiled room in a farmhouse, with its oilcloth-covered table and its rush-bottomed chairs. The officers were out, but on the mantelpiece I found several letters. I opened one from Wyn, to learn that her father was dead. To come back to a letter from her was the nearest approach life held to coming home, and this was a sad homecoming. While I had revelled in four days of ease and rest, counting every moment of pleasure into a fund of profit against whatever losses the future might bring, she had borne days of grief, added to the daily burden of anxiety about me. All that I had won seemed lost at a blow, my comfort and content now stood as treason while she walked in the shadows and my letters from Aire, full of my own good fortune, were struck out of tune.

My next step was clear enough to me, and my immediate task was to persuade my superior officers to my way of seeing. I went to report to the Colonel, and found him at tea. After I had told him what had happened, I asked him if he would support my application for leave. I was already due for leave, but there were more candidates than vacancies. He was sympathetic, and told me to apply, warning me that it would be many days before I could expect to hear the result.

On the next day we moved to Estaires, where we slept the night, and in the morning we moved nearer the line, but not into it. We did not go into the trenches again until five days had passed, and then we found ourselves making a quiet and uneventful journey into a moderately peaceful sector not far from Laventie. Our misfortunes began the next day: the rain came down so heavily and steadily that the side of our trench fell in. We were still in breastworks, and the soil was so wet and marshy that digging was impossible. We lived behind a wall of sandbags filled with mud, with practically no protection against fire or water. Our rampart was not even bullet-proof, and there was not one dug-out that could have withstood a light shell or a heavy shower of rain. There was no lateral buildings of bays to localize the effect of a shell, and there was no parados at our backs. But there was water and mud in plenty, and as the rain fell continuously, the old and rotten sandbags burst, and all hands had to set to to rebuild the walls.

Unless the rain stopped, we were faced with four days of being wet through, and the rain did not stop. One subaltern of my company was ordered to join the Divisional Machine Gun Company, another was wounded, so there were two fewer to walk the deck during the watches. The burden fell heavily on the survivors, and I was more or less continually on duty. We had our share of excitement, for at seven o'clock in the morning, the enemy blew up a mine; the earth rocked, and all the artillery within reach started firing.

Beyond the obvious fact that a mine had been sprung, there was no knowledge of what had happened, but there is an automatic response to all such challenges. I was strolling along the trench towards the dug-out where we ate and slept, wondering how soon breakfast would be ready. The men had been told to stand down and to cook their food. 'Stand-to,' I yelled, and told them to pass the message up the line while I hurried down towards the evil spot; sergeants and corporals dashed away to see their sections, and the company sergeant-major joined me in my rush. It is never pleasant to run towards trouble, but to run into it is worse. Bullets from an enemy machine-gun were ripping the air overhead, sweeping the line of the parapet to catch any heads that stood above it. Shells were bursting in plenty, but as far as I could see, they were doing little damage inside the trench. So we went on, giving a word or two of encouragement as we passed, but dreading all the time to find our progress stopped by a break in the line round the next bay. Soon after passing through the centre of the bombardment we came to the end of my company's sector, thankful that whatever had happened elsewhere, my line was not broken. There I found an officer of the next company and learnt that no damage had been done to his trench. A hurried glance over the parapet showed us the crater of the new mine. The enemy had misjudged the distance, and the crater was in No Man's Land, near an old one in our possession, instead of in our line. Two men had been wounded by shell fire, but not seriously, and as I passed them they made no attempt to disguise their glee at a prospect of a respite from war.

And so to breakfast, on our fourth day in the line. It was still raining, the walls were still falling in, and the water in the trench ran up to the knee. To move about was to wade through a grey-brown soup, feeling with the feet for the duckboards. To miss a duckboard was to dip into another eighteen inches of water. As you walked, your mackintosh trailed behind you and tapped against the corners of the bays; feet and clothes felt heavy, as if they did not belong to you. Another grey day went by, fading slowly into a greyer twilight logged with rain, without a gleam in the sky. About half-past five I was standing, leaning against our sandbag wall, looking towards the Western sky and thinking of tea-time in England, an unfailing source of escape from the troubles of the moment, but bringing with it the sharp-toothed pain of longing.

A signaller came up to tell me that my leave had been granted, and that I was to go down at once to Battalion Headquarters to get my warrant for the journey. As I write them now, the words sound dull and ordinary, but in that wet and gloomy twilight they were highly charged. I hurried back to the company dug-out, rang up the adjutant, and he confirmed this message from another world. He did not know when the leave train left La Gorgue that evening, but he thought that it went early, so there was no time to dawdle.

I summoned the senior subaltern and handed over my command, making no attempt to disguise my hurry. My washing tackle was in a haversack in a corner of the dug-out; I picked it up, took off my revolver and handed it to my servant, and said good-bye to my company officers. I set off down the long, winding communication trench, down the road to England, as I said to myself. Although my feet were on duckboards, awash with the water, my heart was already at home, and life had changed direction. In a few minutes there came a sudden reminder that my heart was too far in advance of my body, for the enemy started shelling the communication trench, thinking no doubt that ration parties would be on their way to the line. I confess that I was seized with panic—to be killed or wounded now, of all times, on my way home to Wyn! I ran, and as I ran I remember hoping that I would meet no one, for how could such an unmilitary progress be justified to the beholder? In my haste I turned too sharply round a corner, missed my footing on the duck-boards, and fell into a pool of muddy water up to my waist. As I was already wet to the skin, this misadventure could not be said to worsen my condition, but it annoyed me intensely at the time, and I walked more warily. What if I slipped again and broke my leg?

I reached Battalion Headquarters and was given my yellow ticket. I had grace enough to thank the Colonel for his kindness, but I grudged every second that stood between me and that train. My mind was obsessed and my judgment warped: every shell that fell within two hundred yards drove terror into me. In my madness I felt sure that the enemy had concentrated the whole purpose of war into one determined attempt to break this journey of mine. War suddenly became real to me, and I was fighting an evil power. I did not dare to let my mind dwell on the prospect before me lest my thinking be made a challenge, to be answered by sudden extinction. Every hazard was magnified into a valley of death. Reason did not triumph fully over this mad racing panic in my brain until I reached the high road, and saw in the groups of men setting about their tasks in a rational and unhurried way, a sign of comfort. They considered themselves to be in safety, so why not I?

Soon I reached houses not yet levelled with the ground, and I met transport going up towards the line with rations for the next day—none for me, praise God!

Then I passed an *estaminet*, and through the open door I could see groups of men talking and laughing. Poor devils, thought I, to find comfort in such trivialities, while I was treading the high road to England. I felt tired and hungry, but I did not dare to stop: it was past seven o'clock, and I could not bear to think of missing that train. I had no clothes for England, I was wet, dirty and unshaved; my shirt and vest were wet, and though I was warm with walking and excitement, I knew that I should be cold later on. Should I try to find the battalion transport lines and change my clothes? No—I might miss the train.

I must have walked eight miles before I

reached the station at La Gorgue. My clothes felt heavy, and even leave sank before a dull sense of hunger and fatigue. It was eight o'clock when I walked into the Railway Transport Officer's office and asked his clerk at what time the leave train left for Boulogne.

'The leave train is cancelled,' said he. I cannot describe the next moment, but my clothes suddenly became heavier and I more tired and hungry. I was about to turn away when he said:

'There is an empty Supply train going down to Boulogne at nine o'clock . . . you can go in that if you like. It's only cattle trucks, and I don't know how long it will be on the journey. Go and tell the guard if you are going in it.'

'Is there a telegraph office anywhere near?' I asked. 'I want to send a wire to England.'

He told me where to find one, and I wired to Wyn to tell her to meet me at an hotel in London the next day. I was about to leave the station to search for a meal when I thought that it would be better to interview the guard. He was a French civilian, and when I asked him how long it would be before his train started, he told me that it was going to start that very minute. I climbed into an empty cattle truck and congratulated myself on my narrow escape; that train was worth more to me than any meal. He was wrong, of course; it was nearly nine o'clock before we started. I walked up and down inside the truck trying to keep warm. It had stopped raining, and the sky was clear. The guard said that he thought it was going to freeze, but I did not believe him. If he was wrong about the time of our starting, he was right about the weather.

We started on the longest journey I have ever known. We stopped at every signal and at every level crossing, but never at a station. I got tired of trying to keep warm and sat down in a corner of the truck, searching my pockets for chocolate, but none was to be found. There was nothing to do but smoke, and that soon palls on an empty stomach. I tried to sleep, but failed; I was too cold. We stopped and shunted, and started again, but never stopped at a station. About three o'clock in the morning my legs and feet began to get numb, while the rest of my body shivered, and I was desperately hungry and tired. It was freezing hard. I found that I could not move my legs—they did not belong to me. At one of our wayside halts I heard the guard passing my truck, so I hailed him. Were we far from Boulogne, or was it possible to stop at a station where we could find an *estaminet?*

We were far from Boulogne, and there was no hope of an *estaminet*.

I told him that I had come straight down from the line after four days and nights of rain, that I had not a dry garment on me, and that I had had nothing to eat or drink since four o'clock the previous afternoon. I was afraid that my feet were becoming frost-bitten. He told me to wait a minute—he would be back soon. He returned, carrying a small box and his lantern, entered the truck and told me to take off my mackintosh and sit on the box. I tried to do this, but I fell over when I attempted to stand. He picked me up and put me to sit on the box, took off my wet mackintosh and wrapped it round my legs. Between my feet he put his lamp, and he told me to sit still without moving until he came back.

In a few minutes the hot air from the lamp began to warm my legs, and I was soon in an agony of pain brought by the returning circulation. In ten minutes I was comfortably warm and in my right mind, saved from frost-bite, pneumonia, and many other evils, thanks to the kind ingenuity of my friendly guard. When I had thanked him, I suggested that if he would persuade the engine driver to stop at a station with an *estaminet* as soon as it was light, we might drink a cup of coffee at my expense. Soon after dawn we drew up at a small station, walked to the door of a café, and hammered at it till a sleepy head peered through a bed-room window to ask what we wanted.

'An English officer in danger of frost-bite—come down and make us a cup of coffee.'

'But there is no fire!'

'Come down and light it.'

Soon the door opened, and we walked into a musty room; a handful of straw in the stove, some wood, and the coffee pot was put on the fire. I called for some cognac, and the guard, driver, fireman, the landlord and myself drank lukewarm coffee, with no sugar, but with plenty of cognac, in the early frost-bound dawn. Life seemed more under our control, and the strong coffee dulled the sense of hunger: leave became a reality once more, and when we reached Boulogne at seven in the morning, the cold and discomfort of the ten-hour journey passed into the limbo of war.

I walked across the railway lines to the officers' club on the quay, washed and shaved, and ate an enormous breakfast. I tried to remove the signs of my slavery, but the mud was drying into my clothes, and the sum total of my exertion was merely to turn my khaki into a yellowish field grey. There was no help for it; I must wait until my mackintosh and breeches were thoroughly dry. My leave had begun, and I abandoned myself to a luxurious effort to catch every second of it, and to stamp every passing hour with an unmistakeable mark of its difference. In the heart a deep pedal note of joy, sustaining all passing moods of semi-anxiety; would Wyn get my wire in time to allow her to reach London to-night—would I be recalled from leave—was it possible that all sailings might be suspended and all ranks returned to their units? These were merely wisps of mist passing between me and the sun. There was no real and lasting challenge to the deep-laid melody of joy racing through my blood; to-day, indeed, Heaven lay before me.

I walked the streets of Boulogne, finding a pleasure in its noise and bustle, in its shops, and in the rubbing of shoulders with people who went home to dinner and who wore slippers of an evening. War was no longer a pre-occupation, it was a disease from which I had recovered. Not even the sad significance of the universal black could penetrate my armour of content; nothing could 'dim the mirror of my joy' that day. I wandered from shop window to shop window, seeking some little present for Wyn, deferring choice from sheer delight in the choosing, until it became a matter of necessity to decide unless I were to reach England empty-handed. I bought a bottle of eau-de-Cologne, finding something of a pleasing symbolism in its fragrance.

Shortly after, I shouldered my haversack and walked down the quay to the boat, forming one of a glad procession, strode up the gangway and went on deck. I met no one I knew, but I did not feel any need of company—who could be lonely on his way home? I leant over the rails and watched the others crowding round the gangway, the soldiers struggling with kit and rifle, and I noticed one soldier carrying two rifles, one German. He was arguing with a sergeant at the foot of the gangway, protesting against the firm order that the German rifle must be left behind. It was a 'souvenir' that he had carried many miles. A Brigadier-General was leaning over the bulwarks and listening to the argument; for the moment it looked as if the soldier's obstinacy would cost him his leave. The General called out gaily, 'Tommy, hand me that rifle.' The soldier stepped to the quay-side and handed the German rifle to the Brigadier. 'Go back to your place and get on to the boat.' The soldier saluted and went back to the foot of the gangway, and came aboard without further ado. As he stepped on deck the General hailed him and gave him back his rifle. 'Look out for me when we come alongside at Folkestone and I'll take it ashore for you.' 'Thank you very much, sir,' said the soldier, as he went away beaming.

It seemed as if we would never sail, but sail we did. As we neared Folkestone, England came in sight, and I realized why poets have sung of those white cliffs; years of my life had slipped away for ever in the five months I had spent in France, and I saw a new country; the train carried us past orchards in blossom; hedges had taken on a new beauty after my sojourn in the pollarded fens of Flanders. The country sang of peace, and every moment was bringing me nearer to Wyn; it would be strange if that journey were not stamped indelibly on my memory. It has now sunk deeper than memory; it has become a part of my being and of my way of thinking.

I reached London at eight o'clock in the evening. For a moment or two I stood outside Victoria station, watching the traffic and drinking in to the full the queer sensation of hearing English spoken by everybody, finding it strange that the inevitable should suddenly be the unexpected. I was in Victoria Street again, where, less than two years ago, I spent my days in a calm and uneventful way of life; I had nothing but memory to warrant my being the same person, and the sharp and bitter discontinuity of war had somehow weakened the belief in this truth. In all that mattered, I was not the same person, a different way of thinking and of feeling had overwhelmed the traces of the old life. The past had become an ancient monument, buried deep, and covered from the mind's eye by the mud of the Low Country. Were my present self to dig in this deposit, it would doubtless discover the remains of the life gone by, but the effort did not seem worth while; better to look forward from the hill-top on which I now stood than to seek the lowlands of 1914, so far away they seemed.

I turned into the hotel and enquired if Wyn had arrived: she had not reached the hotel, so I engaged a room and went upstairs. I called the chambermaid, showed her my clothes, and asked her if she could buy me a new shirt and a pair of socks while I had a bath. In twenty minutes I was clean, and reluctant to put on dirty clothes, so I got into bed and rang the bell. She had not succeeded in finding a shirt, but she gave me a pair of socks she had just finished knitting; I thanked her, and made a note of the number of the room, vowing that if I came back on leave again I would bring her a bottle of eau-de-Cologne to mark my gratitude. Many months after I fulfilled my vow. There was nothing to do but to dress again, and I went down to the lounge to wait for Wyn. Nine o'clock, ten o'clock, passed with no sign of her coming, and I was getting anxious, but at half-past ten she came in through the swing door, with shining eyes, looking pale and slight in her new black clothes. And so, with this meeting, I had reached my 'journey's end'.

IV

MUD

MUD

It was on the 5th May, 1916, that this ten days of delight was destined to end. Our last evening together we spent at some theatre; I have forgotten what we saw, but it is easy enough, even after this long interval of time, to remember the insidious growth of the canker of sadness, and to capture once again the struggle to turn the mind away from the morrow. Six months had passed since we sat in Winchester, on the eve of my first sailing overseas, oppressed by the same burden, and making the same effort to cast it off. Love grows rapidly in the forcing-house of war, and the dull ache of absence fosters a sensitivity and quickens response. The poets have taught us that to mortals endowed with their own delicacy of emotional structure, parting can become an agony of a death, but war, with its rude barbarian violence, had made even of us ordinary creatures, a regiment of sufferers. Common clay as we were, and far enough removed as we thought ourselves from the spun glass of the poet's imagining, we found ourselves betrayed into the very emotions they had sung. That the prose of war should prove the truth of poetry's tale of man's feeling—that it should now be easy to believe that some of those magic lines were indeed a reflection of the real thoughts of real men and women—that was an astonishing discovery. I had read a quantity of poetry, and had even tried to write it, but all with a sense of projecting my personality into an adjacent field of life. Here and now I was treading, at some remove, the very paths the poets had walked before me.

Shortly before eight o'clock in the morning the boat train steamed out of Victoria station, leaving Wyn standing on the platform, one of many women fighting each a lonely battle against a distant peril. Some were to know defeat, others triumph, but none was to escape the rack of doubt and suspense. I cannot tell her tale of that day; the return to an empty room, the quiet packing of a bag, and the cruel sight of other women looking into their husbands' eyes. I saw no beauty in the Kentish orchards that had delighted my eyes but ten days ago, and the flowering hedges were a mockery. If I survived the dangers of war I might once again come home on leave, but many months would have to pass. The 'life' of an infantry officer at the front in those days was very short; it worked out to a mathematical average of a few weeks, fatal or non-fatal wounds came quickly to a junior officer in a line regiment. I had seen many men come and go, and there was little comfort in the prospect before me. There were many officers on the train who were obviously better placed than I—some wonderful difference had raised them to the Staff, but I could see no endowment of mine that could ever serve to take me across the gap that divided the brains of the army from its brawn. My lot was pitched in the mud, and the less I longed for the fleshpots, the better would I be able to eat my bully beef and tinned jam. I had met but few of these higher creatures, nor had I tested their metal, so that it was easy to hold to a belief that my path would never cross their orbit of revolution round that mysterious centre where war was governed. Thus I thought at the time, but destiny was to take me into their midst and to make me one of them, after a close and painful realizing of their human limitations.

On my way home to England, company was a superfluity, and now, on my journey back to France, it would have been an insult to the memory of the wistful glance that followed me overseas. I would go short of many things precious to have and to hold, but I had triumphed over war for ten days. Neither time nor turmoil could deprive me of such riches, garnered and housed, and for ever incorruptible within me. I held the 'perfect sum of all delight'.

In a waking dream I reached Boulogne and unhurriedly searched for my train, almost praying that it had gone. If I had failed to see beauty walking the fields of England that morning, there was little danger of the eye meeting pleasure in France. At ten o'clock I was at the railhead in Merville, and there I spent the night; I had no great desire to remember the journey, and I have forgotten where I slept. My mind was far away. Next morning I walked towards the line in search of my battalion, hoping to find it in reserve; anywhere but in the trenches. I met the transport officer who told me that we were in the trenches in front of Laventie, and that I had arrived just in time for a 'show' that very night. I had come down to earth with a thud, and I was seized with a wild rebellious fear. 'What a plague have I to do with a buff jerkin?' cried Falstaff, and so thought I. It was at such times as this that I pondered grimly on the strange fever that drove me to wrest from an unwilling Government Department permission to enlist in the army.

If any man says that he went into the trenches with indifference, you may brand him a liar. I hated the journey always, but never more than now. Coming straight from the ways of peace, it seemed that I had more to lose, for the deadening power of months of trench habit had been lifted from my mind, leaving my fibre bare to the weakest blast of war. I skulked along a quiet road leading to a few cottages still occupied by peasants, and there I met one of our company commanders. From him I heard the full tale of the coming night. The Corps Commander had decided that German prisoners must be taken, to identify the opposing forces in the sector. The Divisional Commander had selected our brigade for the venture, and the mantle had fallen on him to lead the assaulting party. Men had been picked from the various companies, and a band of adventurers had been kept back from the line to rehearse their assault over a piece of marked ground. My part in the performance was limited. Just before the time fixed for the raid, the whole party would assemble in my company sector. Between the fall of dark and the striking of the hour, I had to see that 'lanes' were cut in our own barbed wire through which the raiders might pass. Our artillery would put down a barrage on the enemy trenches opposite me, to drive the Germans underground and to silence their machine guns. Their task done, the raiding party would dash back to my trenches and then down the communication trench to Battalion Headquarters, leaving me to bear the concentrated fire of the German artillery in the inevitable counter-barrage and retaliation. Simple enough, but I wished that someone else were to play the host that night.

My mental equilibrium thoroughly upset by the prospect of a night of excitement, I took the road once again, steadily descending the scale of civilization from inhabited cottages to isolated ruins, now largely concealed by the budding foliage of May. Soon I came to a straight arrow of road, to all appearances untrodden by man, and all but conquered by the grass advancing from its verges; I had passed the eastern limit of transport, and, in sudden obedience to the bidding of caution I edged to the side of the road. Although I had not walked this way before, I knew well enough that my path would sink in a visible degradation from high road to ditch, and from ditch to an inconspicuous entrance into a communication trench. So it happened. In a few seconds my foot was on a duckboard, on my right hand and left a wall of sandbags, and as the duckboards swung to my tread there rose the unforgettable smell of Flanders mud. It struck chill into the heart, even on this sunny afternoon in late Spring. Here and there a shell burst, with a black cloud in the blue sky to remain as a hideous sign of its menace. Sound, sight and smell were all challenged at once, and they must in concert submit to the degrading slavery of war, chained to a ridiculous chariot heading for utter destruction. Sense and soul were of no account; such ballast might have held the world to a course less futile, but in this mad runaway we had cast sanity to the winds. If ever war was meaningless, it was on this sunny afternoon in May, as I walked slowly on my winding way towards the line. Unheated by recent danger, untired by loss of sleep, judgment was keener and vision was normal; now, as never before, the unrelieved stupidity of this way of manifesting one nation's protest against another filled the mind. War's cruelty, its hideousness and its powers of destruction were to-day overshadowed by its irredeemable idiocy.

Sullen in mood, with a dull dragging at

heart, I reached the front line trench and walked along until I came to the company headquarters' dug-out. In a mechanical way I noticed that the sector was reasonably dry, and that the dug-out was better than the one I had left twelve days ago. I dipped my head, pushed in, and sat down at a table and greeted the officers. Ten minutes passed in exchanging gossip of the line and of London, then tea was brought in. Enamel plates, enamel cups, knives of every pedigree, and the same enamel teapot pouring the same acid tea; a tin of milk, slabs of close-knitted bread, and a tin of non-descript jam. There was little joy in body or mind at the sight of this first meal in the trenches. Within a short twenty-four hours I would succumb to the dull routine of life and would find in any meal a pleasant break, but at the moment I was too lately returned from England, where tea-time brought quiet intimacies by the fireside.

My second in command handed over the copy of battalion orders, and I drove my mind back to the business of the day.

'Have you sent off the situation report?' I asked.

'Yes, it went off an hour ago.'

'What was it?'

'Situation normal, wind south-west.'

I laughed. Those two phrases had become current coin in our intercourse with Battalion Headquarters and had, through long usage, acquired a certain momentum. The odds were that whatever happened during the preceding twelve hours, when the signaller came to say that the situation report was due to go, one would say, automatically, 'Situation normal, wind south-west.' I have written it out before going to sleep, and given it to the signaller with orders to send it off in an hour's time. I have also known the adjutant to ring up indignantly and demand to speak to the officer commanding 'C' Company. 'You say the wind is south-west; 'B' Company on your right say that the wind is north-east. Which is right?'

'Oh, just alter mine to north-east—I expect they are right.'

In theory, the situation report was intended to convey in brief summary the events of the day or night, and the direction of the wind would indicate whether a gas attack was probable. An integration of these reports should acquaint a Divisional Commander with the current history of his command, but I found later in my career that they became fuller as the distance of the writer from the front increased. A touch of east in the wind would cause alarm and despondency in the various commands, and the quick downward communication of such a mood brought irritation to us in the line. Gas-helmets must be ready for immediate use; flannel bags they were in those days, and damnable to wear. To our minds this was sheer fussiness.

It grew dark, and it was time to begin cutting lanes in our wire in front of the point of departure of the raiding party. Our artillery had been engaged during the day in cutting the enemy's wire, lest he should have any doubt where we proposed to attack him. Had we cut the lanes in our wire the night before, the daylight would have underlined our intentions. Soon there began a trickle of men into the trench, with blackened faces and hands, carrying weird weapons. They and the junior officers were shepherded into their proper places with much whispering and shuffling, while the tenants of the trench endeavoured to pursue their normal occupations and to make the normal noises. There was a sense of strain in all, half covered by a spurious excitement. In a desperate silence they climbed over the parapet, hurrying over that small skyline lest the firing of a 'light' pistol should reveal their motion, and taking care that there was no jangling of their equipment. They formed up in a line in No Man's Land, crawling slowly towards the gaps in the enemy wire. Last of all, the officer in command took with him a field telephone on which he could buzz signals back to the artillery liaison officer in the front line. After an eternity of waiting, a buzz announced that the reconnaissance of the wire proved it to be passable; another buzz told us that the party was assembled and ready for the assault. It drew near to the appointed hour, and the seconds dragged unendingly. Watches had been synchronized most carefully.

Zero, a buzz, and then a wild tornado of shell fire. They were off on their journey, inside this three-walled screen of flame. We knew only too well that before many seconds the enemy would add a fourth wall of fire to this screen, and that his wall would rest with its foundation in our trench, but for the moment there was only one orchestra in play. Various coloured lights were sent up from neighbouring sectors of the enemy trenches, and his machine-guns were enfilading No Man's Land. We could, however, hear the bursting of bombs thrown by our men, and we took heart at the sound; they must now be in conflict hand to hand. Then we knew that the enemy artillery had started his barrage, and for the next ten minutes we knew little else. It did not seem possible that any of us could survive this thunderstorm of bursting shells, but strangely enough we suffered little. The barrages and the machine-gun fire died down to spasmodic outbursts, and our men began to trickle back to our line—some of them, for many never came back. We could get no coherent account of what had happened, but it was clear that their visit was not unexpected. Two officers did not return. Now began an anxious and laborious task; we sent our patrols to scour No Man's Land in search of our wounded and dead. The search lasted all night, with diminishing success, and during the following day we scanned through our peep-holes and periscopes for any sign of our men, but we found none.

When the varying accounts of the survivors were collated and the final count was made, it became evident that we had paid dearly for the assault—no prisoner, dead or alive, came into our hands. Sadness fell upon us all, officers and men, for there were many friends we would never see again, and the reaction from the excitement of the night brooded over the whispering groups, assessing the ultimate value of the enterprise and finding it not worth the cost.

In the evening we heard a shout from No Man's Land, and I sent out a patrol to investigate: they brought back one of our men, slightly wounded, who had spent the long day waiting for the night, but he seemed little the worse for his exposure.

This epilogue ended, we turned again to our daily task of unending displacement of mud. We filled sandbags with it, piled them up into a wall, beat them into a firm rampart, there to remain until a shell-burst undid our efforts. Then our damaged wall would sag and drop, and our labour in lifting mud three or four feet above its original resting place was made waste. All our elaborate rearrangement of mud—for our task was nothing more than this—was born to be defeated; our triumph over mud was short-lived and highly localized. Here and there we used hurdles, but hurdles had to be carried up long and winding communication trenches, and there are few burdens more difficult to handle on a dark night, with feet slipping on the slime-covered duckboards. If ever a party of men struggled up towards the line carrying these unwieldy loads, it was doomed to meet a descending file of fellow-sufferers bearing some ungainly and unmanageable freight. As infantry we were but hewers and drawers in any matter concerning trench architecture. The Engineers were our masters, and wisdom would die with them. When we had laboured all night to build a wall of sandbags, and had rammed hard at the middle to conceal a bulge that threatened to reveal our lack of science, a wise sapper would in the morning tell us that here, of all places, common sense would have indicated a hurdle. If we tried to turn this lesson to advantage and used hurdles in our next building, it was with no surprise that we heard that hurdles were useless in such emergencies. Whatever we did was wrong, or at best, it merited no more than the condescending recognition that as amateurs we could not in reason be held accountable to the standards of the sappers. The Engineers were large employers of labour, and we were the labour; they were capitalists, with their enormous stores of material, and we were the proletariat who had to carry these stores on our backs. How could they be loved of the infantry?

I wrote some doggerel verse that gained a considerable notoriety at the time, as it was reprinted in one of the illustrated weekly papers —it reflected the mood of the day. Here is some of it:

Sing a song of sandbags,
Fill them up all day,
Build them up at nightfall,
At dawn they slide away.
When the sapper sees them,
He'll have a lot to say,
'Why didn't you use hurdles?'
'Oh . . . run away and play!'

Day followed day with little to mark the eve from the morrow. Fear, boredom, boredom, fear—we swung from one to the other, with a growing fatigue as we drew nearer to the night of relief, and our minds became as muddied as our clothes.

When anything happened to revive our attention, it formed a topic of long discussion and minute examination. One day a German deserter came into our line. He was surrounded by eager questioners, but he could speak no English, and none of us knew German. His pockets were searched hurriedly by the curious, and I arrived in time to see that no letters or papers of any military value were taken from him: a few mark notes and some cigarettes were treasure enough for my company. Someone gave him a biscuit, another a slice of bully beef, and in a few minutes he had more cigarettes than he could smoke in a day. 'You're a lucky blighter, Fritz, not 'arf you ain't,' was the burden of their song. He seemed to be puzzled at this cordiality in a language he did not understand, as if he had expected hard words and blows. I sent him under escort to Battalion Headquarters, and saw him no more, but for many days I heard critical discussions of his clothing and boots, ending in unanimous recognition of their superiority over ours. His boots were better than ours, better fitted for trench life, but I could see no great merit in his clothes. There was endless argument, and his coming was no less a service to us than a betterment of his own condition.

We were not without other visitors, but they generally brought trouble in their wake. Every day, and sometimes more than once a day, the Colonel would inspect his battalion front. No one knew the hour of his coming. Nothing escaped that keen eye of his—bad duckboard here, there a weakening in the wall, fire-step to be repaired in one bay, two men had dirty rifles, one man did not know where company headquarters stood, three men did not know where to find the ammunition boxes, and one lance-corporal seemed doubtful where the gas alarm was situated. He would enter our dug-out, take out his note-book, and begin his chronicle of shortcomings. The law of average must hold, and there must have been occasions when he asked a man of normal intelligence where the bombs were stored, and heard the simple truth told without hesitation, but I was never made aware of such strokes of good fortune. I knew only too well that if the Colonel must ask a searching question, it would be hurled at the most stupid man in the company.

He was a good officer, and a kindly man, who concealed his feelings in spurts of sharp and sudden sentences.

'Get that parapet higher, d'ye see?'

'Yes, sir.'

'No good tinkering at the bay, see? Rebuild it.'

'Yes, sir.'

'Don't like that bomb-store, d'ye see?'

'Yes, Colonel.'

'Dam dirty rifle one fellow had: jump on his sergeant, see?'

'I will, sir.'

'Well, I must be going on. . . . No thanks, I won't have a drink. . . . Good morning.'

In the nature of things, there can be little cordiality between a Colonel and his junior officers in war time, but we respected him and liked him, and felt that his brusque ways were not the whole of the man. There was an underlying sympathy with a young man bearing a heavy burden of responsibility, though it was well concealed on a morning parade when we were out of the line. He was considerate in small things; once only did I know him to accept an offer of whisky and water in a company dug-out in the trenches, on a day of sweltering heat, and then he looked at the bottle to see how much we had before he accepted. He declined our hospitality on many occasions when he was obviously tired, from an unselfish disinclination to impoverish us. If on his visit he found the company commander asleep, he would not let him be disturbed: greater men than he were not so considerate.

The Brigadier was a daily plague. He had won the Victoria Cross and the Distinguished Service Order in the South African War. He was slight, athletic in build, and good-looking: his mind was slow in working, but tenacious to the point of obstinacy. He spoke slowly, in a prim way—his fellow regular officers called him 'Jane'. It would be a misuse of words to call him brave, but he was certainly fearless. I have heard an uncharitable company commander, labouring under a grievance, say that he was too stupid to be frightened of anything but reason. He took a delight in exposing himself to fire, quite forgetting that the infantry officer who was his unwilling companion was being forced into a foolhardy challenge of the powers that troubled him day and night, when the Brigadier was far away from the line. He had little sense of humour, but I once saw him laugh at an incident that might have brought trouble upon my head.

It was a cold and wet night, and I was following him along my sector, listening to an interminable catalogue of minor faults. We came to a Lewis Gun post, and as we approached it the gunner fired a drum of ammunition. He did not recognize the General, who asked him:

'Was it you firing then?'

'Yes.'

'What were you firing at?'

'Don't know.'

'Then why did you fire?'

'Just to bloody well amuse myself,' said the stubborn Welsh collier, in his close-clipped South Wales speech. The General turned away and laughed, to my great relief.

In these days his great preoccupation was the removal of tins. All tins were to be buried behind the line, and woe to the company commander if the General found an empty tin in a trench—he was damned for the day. When the news of his coming sped before him, corporals and sergeants forsook the superintending of military tasks for a wild drive of forgotten tins into a hasty burial in the mud beneath the duck-boards. Great was the urgency of concealing such indecencies if peace were to reign during his visit. Fundamentally he was right in his struggle for sanitation, but to us it seemed as if this admittedly worthy enterprise were of secondary importance compared to the strengthening of our protection against shell fire. Any improvement in the parapet, or parados when it existed, was sure to gain approval, but there was a queer reluctance to encourage the building of better dug-outs for our comfort and our safety at times when more war was waged against us than we were waging.

It seemed to us that our superiors did not inwardly admit that comfort was desirable, or that any one should seek to be in a dug-out if the enemy were shelling the line. I may be wrong. The real reason may have been that we were short of supplies, and not that the true British spirit of waging war was to scorn any perfectioning of our present position because we would in a day or two, according to the theory, be driving the enemy out of his trenches. We lost an army corps of men through inadequate protection from shell fire, and from diseases brought on by unnecessary exposure, but as they would in all probability have been murdered on the Somme, it might have made little difference in the sum of things. The enemy took great trouble to build strong and comfortable shelters for his men, while we were content with hasty improvisations but rarely rain-proof.

The Brigadier wore a mackintosh jacket over his uniform, a pair of mackintosh trousers over his breeches, and a steel helmet that tended to slide over his left ear. There was no visible mark of rank at first, but later he fixed on his helmet the crossed sword and baton. His real badge of office was a wooden staff exactly four feet six inches long, and with this he tested the height of the top layer of sandbags on the parapet over the fire-step. It was decreed that this height of four feet six inches must never be exceeded—there was little danger of any shortage, but a tall man standing on the fire-step felt acutely conscious of his upper eighteen inches. This mackintoshed figure, with boyish face and pouting expression, conscientiously measuring his staff against the trench wall, and finding a quiet satisfaction in the rare tallying of the two heights, commanded a force of three thousand men. In the stagnant condition of our war-making, it might be said that though he was the titular head of this body, to which he issued orders, he commanded no one. He elaborated for our benefit orders he had received from above, but he was no prime mover. He led no one, nor did he ever taste the thrill of throwing mass against mass. We were tenants of an estate of mud, and he was high bailiff, holding us to a careful tenancy, meticulous even in his over-seeing of our domestic economy. He was zealous in his administration, sparing not him-self, nor others, struggling manfully with a burden that appeared to us to be a little too large for his capacity, and concealing this by an untiring expenditure of physical energy.

On rare occasions we were 'at home' to more distinguished visitors. The Divisional Com-mander, Staff Officers of the Division and Corps would move quietly and quickly through our trench in the early morning. We knew them not, save by their red tabs and badges of rank, but they asked no awkward questions and were easily entertained. They did not seem to belong to our army. We noticed that they were cir-cumspect in their choice of day and time for such a venture, and we envied them their short sojourn in our wilderness. The lines that follow were written on one such occasion, and I see now that they are but a reflection of the immemorial contempt of the infantry:

> There they go round the company front
> To see the poor devils that bear the brunt
> Of ev'ry strafe and trench mortar stunt,
> On a dull and misty morning.
>
> What if the Hun should see them come?
> They'd vanish as soon as my tot of rum,
> But well do they know that the guns are dumb
> On a dull and misty morning.

When our four days in the front line came to an end, we marched to excellent billets in a little village called Laventie. The houses had suffered, and here and there were blotches of destruction, but several of the inhabitants had remained to trade with the soldiers. We had beds, and a comfortable mess-room in a small house with a pretty garden at the back, possibly the very garden that tempted Wyndham Tennant to write the poem called 'Home Thoughts from Laventie'. The name of this village has a music of its own. We found kindness there, rest and cleanliness. Another battalion of my regiment was near us, though in the line, and I met my young brother many times. He was a private soldier, happy and proud of his task as battalion orderly and messenger. We were separated by the ocean of rank and discipline, but whenever I saw him in Laventie I smuggled him into the house, gave him a bath and a change of underclothing, and a tremendous meal followed by a cup of coffee—great luxuries to him, and now a cherished memory to me of brightness carried into a young life doomed to end so quickly.

The month of May drew towards its end with little to differentiate one spell of trench duty from another, but during one of our periods of rest I was selected by the Brigade to carry out a billeting reconnaissance. This took me four days to do, and though I have forgotten what I did, I still remember the feeling of self-importance that filled me as I started out on the task. Could it be that I was destined to use my brain in the service of our campaign, instead of my legs and arms? I could not say, and I dared not hope, but after six months of the trenches I would count any other service freedom. Some men found work to do where no danger shadowed them, where mud was not their master, so why not I? This was an uneasy ferment to lie in the mind of a company commander in the infantry; better for him to be content with a parapet for a horizon, to keep his imagination grey as the soil around him, and to indulge in no longing to join the aristocracy of war. No captain of foot could hope to survive the war if he were tied to the trenches day in and day out. His hope of salvation lay in a disabling wound, or in selection for work elsewhere, before the length of his days came to a sudden end.

I wondered how I had escaped from death or disablement in spite of six months' service at the front, but optimism was checked by the thought that we had not yet taken part in an open battle. That would come soon enough, bringing with it a quick assessment of my fate. I hoped, with many others, that I might find myself chosen to play a part of greater significance and of less danger than our daily drudgery. But I had no grounds for my hoping. I buoyed myself up with the thought that if I proved faithful in a little thing, such as a billeting reconnaissance, I might find greatness thrust upon me some day.

Shortly afterwards the adjutant fell sick on the eve of our going into the trenches, and I was summoned by the Colonel to take up his duties during his absence. Another stirring up of the fancy, and I saw in it a sign and a portent. Set down in cold blood, my claims to recognition as a budding Staff Officer were matter for laughter. First, and most mirth-provoking, I had organized and carried out a Brigade cookery class: second, I had made a billeting reconnaissance for the Brigade: third, I was chosen by the Colonel to replace the adjutant during the latter's absence. More metal than this was required to forge a Staff Officer! But I did not allow this to diminish my present joy in the work of a locum tenens. I took pride in adding every new experience to my equipment, and I learnt with some surprise that the amenities of life at Ebenezer Farm—the strange name of our Battalion Headquarters—were more pleasant than our reports had suggested. There was a tablecloth and crockery, and the meat was properly cooked. In the line our meat was fried to a uniform toughness, made palatable only by the sauce of our hunger.

Closer acquaintance with the Colonel ripened my respect for him: I saw him at his ease, writing letters to his wife, vexed because the post had brought him no letters from England, grumbling at the shortage of butter—I saw him as a man with other men. I heard him argue with the Brigade Major, defending the battalion against some threatening calumny, and I learnt that his peace was as open to interruption as that of any company commander. It may be said that any man of imagination should have known this, even if he did spend his days in the mud, but I can only answer that we did not exercise our imagination beyond the boundaries of our small parish in the trenches. There may have been junior officers who studied the course of the war at large, but I was not of their number. There was evil enough on my company front to satisfy my curiosity, and a certain callousness would permit a man of ordinary humaneness to show no concern at the afflictions of his neighbour company. Now, however, I had to enlarge my mind to the conception of a battalion of four companies; education was being thrust upon me. I was soon to relapse to my parochialism, for the adjutant recovered and returned to duty, and I reverted to my old and narrow task. My second in command probably felt a similar shrinking in his world when he went back to his platoon on my coming.

I found my company in reserve billets at Riez Bailleul. It is enough to say of this hamlet that we slept between sheets, and that it seemed pleasant to the feet to tread upon a hard road, free from the downward tug of mud. It was nearly eleven o'clock at night before the company was safely tucked away in the big barns. A hundred men are a hundred possibilities of error to a company commander: naked lights, lost equipment, to-morrow's programme, men to go away to attend courses, wiring parties for strong points behind the line, fuel for the cooker —these and a score of other matters are projected on to the screen of the mind as slides from some powerful lantern, demanding each its quota of time and attention from a tired brain. To-morrow the pack of men will be reshuffled; zealous corporals will discover better dwelling places for their sections, and the farmer's wife will be protesting with vigour against some proposed encroachment upon a storing place reserved for farm use, quoting the 'Etat Major' and threatening us with the 'Mairie', but to-night there is no desire strong enough to conquer every man's craving for rest and sleep.

The Company Sergeant-Major and I turned at last to the farmhouse and walked through the kitchen into the little room beyond. The shutters are drawn, and a hanging oil lamp throws a yellow light on the faded walls. The stained and hacked American cloth nailed down on the top of the three-legged wooden table looks bright and clean to-night, and the red tiled floor shows here and there a glow of colour between the piles of equipment, gas-helmets and raincoats thrown carelessly upon it. Enamelled cups on the table, and a half-finished bottle of whisky, letters and newspapers to show that the mail has arrived, two subalterns sitting astride rush-bottomed chairs with jackets unbuttoned and Sam Browne belts hanging over one shoulder, reading their letters and opening parcels, one of them young enough to be eating sweets at this time of night. The sergeant-major shuts the door leading to the kitchen, and we both sit down wearily.

In private life he is a London school teacher: tall and thin, with a firm mouth and a determined eye, untiring and unmovable. The war seems to hold no surprises for him, either good or bad, and it is as if its plan were revealed to him, leaving him powerless to do aught but to acquiesce in its slow unfolding. If two words sufficed to make clear his meaning, to add a third would be to court confusion, so his words were few. His face showed plainly his amused tolerance of the idiosyncrasies of impetuous or lethargic subalterns, and I felt that in his thinking there were but two men in the company not entirely bereft of common sense, and that I was the second. Our life thrust us close together; his position was in its way as solitary as my own. He also had to keep firm in his mind a critical assessing of the worth of his friends in varying emergencies, and a sober valuation of men whom he did not like. I owe a great deal to Ford, and I regret that I have never met him since I left the battalion; there were many conversations, begun on our long marches as we walked together at the head of the company, that called for a finishing in times of peace.

I poured out two pegs of whisky and passed him the water—there was never any soda in our mess—while one of the subalterns offered him a cigarette, but he and I preferred to smoke a pipe on such an occasion of ease. Gossip of the line followed. Had I heard what Delivett said when a pip-squeak blew some mud into his mess-tin, and of his long search for a clean sandbag with which to wipe his rasher of bacon afterwards? Corporal Young's brother had been sent home at once to work on munitions as soon as they found that he was an oxy-acetylene welder, and there was a threatened epidemic of welding ability in the company as soon as this was known, until the sergeant-major had pointed out that the welders were tested in France before they were sent home. A score of other little snapshots of the moving life of a body of men followed, most of them depicting incidents unknown to the least unapproachable of company commanders, unguessed at in spite of the close contact of life in the trenches.

The first day in reserve billets was devoted to a spring-cleaning of man, his apparel and his gear, and to the making up of small deficiencies. One of the officers would ride over to the Field Cashier, borrowing a horse or a bicycle, and the men were given an advance of pay. Letters were written, *estaminets* were filled with groups of eager gossiping soldiers, and aimless strolling about, half in search of friends in other companies, half in escape from the enforced contact of stationary life, gave to everybody a pleasant sense of freedom. There was at this time little or no long-range shelling, and our four miles from the line warranted an unconcern at the progress of war. No aeroplane dropped bombs on these hamlets, nor did our guns break the silence of the night. On the evening of our first day of rest, a distant thunder of artillery fire, long sustained, and occasionally breaking out into a furious roll, forced itself on our incurious ears: vague wonderings and dim suspicions that something out of the ordinary give-and-take of trench bombardment was afoot grew into conviction that an attack was in progress. As it began to grow dark I walked out along the road and saw the ripple of flashes in the Eastern sky. Suddenly a bugle sounded the Alarm.

I ran back to the farmyard to find everybody tumbling into equipment and picking up rifles, while the non-commissioned officers hurried back and fro from the barn to the alarm-post, shepherding the men into order and calling over the rolls of their sections. There was so much to be done at the moment that there was little time to think. Had every man got his gas-helmet, his bandoliers of ammunition and his iron ration of food? Had the bombers bombs, and the Lewis Gun section their spare drums of ammunition? Who left that light burning in the barn? . . . Parade by platoons on the road, two deep and well to the side. . . . The cooker could follow later, with the transport . . . the adjutant wants to speak to the company commander. . . .

Gradually order triumphed over the welter of things to be done, each more urgent than the other, and in less than fifteen minutes the company was on the road, ready to move, while at the door of the farmhouse stood the civilian inhabitants, stolidly wondering why this turmoil had broken in upon their evening of coffee selling. The moon rose over the tall poplars, and the bark of a dog sounded sharply against the background of whispering in the ranks.

There was now time to think, and to speculate on the hundred possibilities of the night. To plod our way back to the trenches we left twenty-four hours ago, to lose three whole days of peace in this quiet hamlet, to form up in some half-derelict breastwork before launching a counter-attack—whatever else the night might bring, it could not fail to bring us these. Was this the beginning of a new German offensive, and were we to be thrown haphazardly into a torrent that could not carry us anywhere but to destruction? Why could not the men in the trenches hold their own? We had called upon no one while we held the gate . . . devil take them! Not a man felt that this was his time to give another stroke for his country, nor that his road would lead him to help a hard-pressed comrade. Walking up and down in front of the double line of men, I could hear nothing but grumbling. The flashes were still rippling across the Eastern sky. Some vowed that the disturbance was well to the south of our Divisional sector, others were equally confident that the Duck's Bill crater was the centre of the struggle.

The Colonel arrived; his first words were lost in the noisy jumping to attention and shouldering of arms, but I gathered that the adjutant was still trying to find out why we were in this state of alarm.

'Have your Lewis Gun men got their spare drums and their ammunition?'

'Yes, sir.'

'I've just found out that the Battalion's spare drums are empty. Empty, d'ye see? Dam bad business, dam bad. What's the name of that corporal?'

'Brown, sir.'

'Damned untidy fellow!'

'Are we to stay here till orders come, sir?'

'Yes, stay where you are, but send an orderly to Battalion Headquarters to bring any messages. . . . The men can stand easy. . . .'

An hour passed, while we waited impatiently for some sign, but none came. We grew cold and weary, and our equipment began to pull down our shoulders in spite of all the hitching up, we began to feel hungry, and eager discussion about the unpleasantness of our immediate future gave way before the rising tide of our present discomfort. Better anything than this endless waiting. Suddenly an orderly dismounted from his bicycle, saluted and blurted out, 'Colonel's orders, sir . . . [here a pause for breath and a quick swallow] . . . Company is to stand down and go back to the billets. Parade to-morrow morning as usual.'

I turned round to the subalterns, gave the order to dismiss by platoons and walked away, back to the farmhouse. So this was the end of that eternity of waiting! We never found out exactly what happened to cast this stone into our quiet pool; all that we could glean was that a very heavy bombardment of our trenches had caused our commanders to see in it the prelude to a large scale attack. We had lost more than an evening's quiet: gone for ever was that sense of inviolable security that had hitherto brooded over our days of rest in reserve. The hand of war had left the trenches to pillage our bedroom, an outrage we found hard to forgive, a breaking of a gentleman's bargain. There were trenches, and there were rest billets, and the rhythmic alternation between one and the other had emphasized their difference into an absolute cleavage. The era of systematic and determined long range shelling had not yet begun, neither was there any aeroplane bombing of back areas, so that two or three miles were sufficient to separate war from peace. We were to look back later upon these months of early 1916 as a time of peace, marked by a gentlemanly observance of the decencies of life at the front, when the Western end of a communication trench was the beginning of the Eastern outposts of civilization, but this night we went to sleep in an angry mood of resentment at such a disturbance of our privacy.

V

ALARMS AND DIVERSIONS

ALARMS AND DIVERSIONS

FLUELLEN: Tell you the duke, it is not so good to come to the mines, for, look you, the mines is not according to the disciplines of the war: the concavities of it is not sufficient; for, look you, th' athversary, you may discuss unto the duke, look you, is digt himself four yard under the countermines, by Cheshu, I think a' will plow up all, if there is not better directions. *King Henry V*, iii, 2.

EARLY in June we went back to the front line, to the sector we knew so well. A warm and sunny day had dwindled to a quiet evening when we paraded on the roadside, a day of little work and much lounging. Many letters had been written and censored, the barns had been tidied, and the last of the stray tins was now in the incinerator; while the men stood gossiping in the ranks, the Company Sergeant-Major and I tramped silently in and out of the barns and the farm buildings on our final tour of inspection. We could find no sign of damage in our tenancy, but our hostess would follow with keener eye, and there would doubtless be a claim for some petty deterioration of an all but derelict farm. There was little need to talk, for there was nothing new to say. Twilight came, and the dusk, bringing with them a minor third into the key of our mood, while the tramp of feet on the road rang like the ticking of a clock to mark the slipping away of wasted time, hours that might have added to the true wealth of life, sunk instead into a morass of futile slavery. Every stride took us away from the simple pleasures of our local peace, of our temporary escape from the degradations of mud: the faint glow in the sky and the brooding stillness of the green earth conspired to sharpen the ache in each man's heart.

Our line strung out as we broke into sections, then into file, until we found our feet shuffling over the duckboards of the communication trench. It was dark, but the occasional firing of a Very light threw its unreal and harsh glare over the pitted landscape. We reached the line, and were greeted eagerly by the tired men who were waiting for us, waiting to return to the very barns we had left. There was little warmth in our answer. I had walked ahead of my company, and I pushed past the small groups in the fire-bays until I came to the dug-out where the officers sat, fully dressed and ready to cut to the shortest of words and time the formalities of handing over the command of the sector.

'I'm leaving you this candle, Griff, and there's some rum in this bottle.'

'Thanks for the candle, but why didn't you get rid of your own rum! You know what a nuisance and a responsibility it is to have so much of it about. . . . Good-night! I hope we have as quiet a time as you did. How's the Duck's Bill crater?'

'Just as it was—quiet enough. . . . Good luck to you! . . .'

We began badly. One of my subalterns took out a patrol to scour the slopes of the crater, to make sure that the enemy had not secured a hiding place on its Eastern face. The message was passed along the line: 'Patrol going out to the Duck's Bill from one o'clock till two,' and all was quiet save the stammer of a Lewis Gun firing at the enemy's rear lines to conceal our lack of activity. Soon we heard a bomb bursting in No Man's Land, then many more in quick succession: the enemy did not fire, neither did we, lest the wrong men be hit. All was darkness, for the same reason. The flashes showed that the tussle was pitched near the crater, but after a dozen bombs were thrown, silence came again. There was nothing to do but wait until our patrol returned: ten minutes, twenty minutes passed slowly by with no whisper from the other side of the barbed wire, although most of the men were on the fire-step, peering and listening. I became uneasy in my mind and decided to go out in search of our patrol, taking one man with me. Revolver in hand, I crept out of our trench and felt my way through the wire, crawling in the direction of the crater and halting frequently to listen for any sound of our returning patrol. The night was very dark and still, magnifying every rustle of our clothes against the long grass into a malevolent hiss. We came to the crater, but found no challenge to our progress, so we clawed our way up its clayey side and stared into the cavity. Nothing seemed to move within this cauldron, and all was silent. Just as I stepped over this little sky-line, the enemy fired a Light pistol. From an enveloping blackness I broke into a world of light: my shadow seemed enormous as it crawled in the wake of the falling star above; my body grew into that of a giant as I stood still, watching my shadow, and I felt myself a target for every bullet within half a mile of me. I was terror stricken: I was naked to all the peering world. Would that light never flicker and fail? Why had I not been shot? My breath came quickly, and my mouth grew dry in an instant. I dared not move, not an arm nor a leg, although there seemed a paradise of security in the hollow at my feet. As a statue I might live; if I moved, I was dead. Dead, dead—the evil thought rang as a tolling bell in my head, and there would be a wild crash of pain. Now, at this instant of my thinking, there was a finger on a trigger, and a yard of steel moving slowly to choose the very point of my agony. The long seconds dragged themselves to an end, and the ball of fire dropped to the ground with a hiss: darkness rushed in to drown this will-o'-the-wisp, and I threw myself over the edge of the crater into safety. A few minutes later we crept through a sap into our own line, now become a blessed protection against the dangers lurking beyond this sand-bagged wall. My first question was a sign that I was back again in my normal world of responsibility for others. . . . Yes, it had returned, after a bombing scrap with an enemy patrol, with no losses or hurt.

Just as a parent scolds a child who has narrowly escaped hurt, relieving his own anxiety by pointing a moral, and disguising his inward relief in reproof, so did I curse my subaltern because he did not return immediately to the line to report the result of his encounter. In my heart I was cursing that unknown German sentry who had fired a 'light' pistol at the very moment of my crossing a miniature hill-top, but my words were hurled at my subaltern. I damned all craters and all the devices of mining, drank half a cupful of rum, and stretched my legs on the floor of the dug-out for my two hours of sleep.

If the enemy digs a mine, we must dig another, and if we can dig below him and blow up our mine before he is ready to spring his, we have done well. If we can delay our springing until his is charged with explosive, our victory will become a triumph. A miner, though he works unseen, cannot conceal his work. The spoil that he carries from his mine has a clayey blueness easily distinguishable from the mud of the surface, and the sound of his pick travels through the ground into the tunnel where his rival is listening, and is magnified by a geophone—a kind of stethoscope—into clear audibility. The entrance to our mine stood at the end of my company's sector, just outside its boundary. An Australian Tunnelling Company was responsible for this enterprise, easy prey to bantering queries from our men as to how their mothers were getting on down below, and when they were coming back from leave. Its commanding officer frequently walked along my sector on his way to the communication trench, and I learned from him, with much relief, that there was no suspicion of any mining in my territory, and with equal relief, that it would be some time before our mine would be ready for springing. I had suffered from mines at Givenchy, and I wished them all to the devil that prompted such inhuman and murderous devices.

On our second day in the line, a keen-eared sergeant reported that he had heard suspicious sounds in a certain fire-bay midway along our sector; he was a South Wales miner, and he was convinced that the sound was that of a pick at work underground. The adjutant decided to join us in our investigation, so we went to the threatened fire-bay to sit down and listen. I could hear nothing, but the adjutant thought that he could, so we listened again with our ears on the duckboards. There was a faint recurring sound. I went to the adjoining sector to look for the expert, and when I returned with the Australian subaltern, he also thought that there was a suspicious sound.

This was a disturbing business: we had no mine near this spot, and before we could countermine, the enemy could blow us up at his own choosing. I was ordered to move all the men out of this fire-bay and the bays on either side, to post a Lewis Gun team on each side of the threatened area, and to occupy a half-derelict trench some thirty yards to the rear with a garrison strong enough to repel any attack when the front line had been blown up. We spent a dismal night waiting, and I admit that I hurried through this deserted part of our front line during my patrolling of our sector. The time most favoured for touching off a mine was at stand-to in the early dawn, when the whole garrison was under arms and filling the bays, and this cargo of clay could take with it to destruction the greatest number of lives. Dawn broke slowly this morning, but the day came at last, and we saw in a thin column of smoke rising from the German trenches a sign of safety. He was cooking his breakfast; if he could start the day in normal fashion, so could we, and we turned to our ordinary tasks, relieved for another twenty-four hours from this wearying burden of anxiety.

In the afternoon I met the commander of the tunnelling company, and we sat down on the duckboards in the fire-bay, listening carefully. There was undoubtedly a faint noise, not unlike the echo of a distant tapping, somewhat hollow, and irregular in rhythm. He listened with his geophone, tapping the walls, and the floor of the trench, and the fire-step, in his endeavour to localize the origin of this mysterious sound. The instrument did not seem to magnify the noise. We were all confounded, and there was much discussion of technical matters beyond my comprehension.

I walked about, thinking. If the geophone did not magnify this throbbing, the sound must have an origin above ground. But there were no wires, nothing to make an Æolian harp; besides, the sound was low in pitch. I stood in one corner of the bay, leaning against the sand-bagged wall of the trench, pondering idly while the tunnellers were investigating. Below my left hand, resting on the fire-step, there was an empty rum jar. Suddenly a thought flashed through my mind with all the vividness of an inspiration.

'Can you hear the noise now?' I asked.

'Yes, faintly, but quite definitely.'

'So can I,' I answered.

I changed my position slightly, and in an inconspicuous and apparently aimless way, I put the palm of my hand on the mouth of the rum jar, stopping the orifice.

'Can you hear it now?' said I.

'No, I don't think so—keep still a few moments while we listen. . . . No, I can hear nothing.'

I agreed—I could hear nothing. I took my hand away, and the noise recurred. On some pretext or another I caused the experiment to be repeated, until I was satisfied.

'Here is your mine,' I said, pointing to the rum jar. They looked at me in astonishment, frankly incredulous. We all bent our heads and listened carefully, crowding round the rum jar: a faint and hollow booming was clearly heard, but when I put my hand on the mouth of the jar, it stopped abruptly. I placed my lips near the mouth and blew across it; the faint and hollow sound grew into a recurrent booming, and as I blew more strongly, gave place to the deep note of the jar. I picked up the jar and placed it in the next fire-bay, in the same position. There was silence in our bay, but a faint sound in the next. The wind, as it came round the corner, blew across the mouth of the jar, and the gusts made the sound recur.

We went away laughing, our anxiety dissolved into ridicule, and the 'rum jar mine' became a regimental joke. All that remained to be done was to cancel our elaborate precautions for the defence of the sector, and in an hour the fire-bays were once more inhabited; the empty jar was broken and buried with mock solemnity in a shell hole. This 'mine' at any rate, was not 'according to the disciplines of the war'.

Delivett carried with him, even into the crowded warren of the trenches, a silence that made him seem a stranger. He had served with the battalion from the start, but he was little given to any conversation beyond the need of the moment. He had no tales to tell in billet or in dug-out. No one knew his age, no one knew whether Delivett was his real name. In spite of the figure standing opposite his name and regimental number, describing him as thirty-four in 1914, it was obvious that he had forgotten his first fifteen years when he gave that answer to the Recruiting Officer. He said that he had not served in the Army prior to the War, but there were times when his carriage brought a doubt to the mind.

Short in stature, and stockily built, with a smile weaving in and out of the lines of his face, never actually smiling, but always on the point of giving way; even when he slept there was a curious curving of the corners of his mouth, as if he were struggling not to laugh. I have forgotten what occupation he claimed in civil life, but it was so impossible to reconcile with his bearing that no one cared to question him about it. He wrote no letters that came to the officers to be censored; he may have found a Field Service Postcard with 'I am well', an ample link between him and his kin. Perhaps the occasional issue of a green envelope for uncensored letters, too rare an issue for most men, was frequent enough to satisfy him. He strutted along the duckboards, pipe in mouth, head in the air, hailed by everybody as he passed, and slowly removing his pipe to spit before he threw over his shoulder some quiet monosyllabic reply.

Towards the end of May, a dozen recruits joined the company, young reinforcements, boyish and slight. Early one morning the enemy began to shell the trench with whizz-bangs; it was a sudden angry storm, too fierce and too localized to last long. I had just passed the fire-bay in which Delivett was frying a rasher of bacon, with five of these lads watching him and waiting their turn to cook. I stopped in the next bay to reassure the others. Suddenly a pale and frightened youth came round the corner, halting indecisively when he saw me, turning again, but finally going back reluctantly to his fire-bay in despair of finding any escape from his trap. Between the crashes of the bursting shells a high-pitched sing-song soared up.

'You'll 'ev 'em all over,' . . . *Crash*. . . .'All the milky wuns.' . . . *Crash*. . . .'All the milky coconuts. . . .' ' . . . You'll 'ev 'em all over. . . . All the milky wuns.' . . . *Crash*. . . .'Ther-ree shies a penny. . . . All the milky coconuts. . . . You'll 'ev 'em all over.' . . . *Crash*—and then silence, for the morning hate ended as suddenly as it began.

I walked to find Delivett still frying bacon, and the five youths smiling nervously, crouched below the firestep. I sent them away on some improvized errand and faced Delivett.

'That's a fine thing you did then, Delivett,' I said. He looked up, mess-tin lid in his hand, saying nothing, but the lines round his mouth moved a little.

'You saved those lads from panic—they were frightened out of their wits,' I added.

'Yes sir, they was real scared,' he replied.

'Delivett, you've spent a lot of time on Hampstead Heath.'

'Yes sir. . . . I ran a coconut shy there once. . .'

With these words a man and an environment fused into a unity, satisfying and complete in itself; here at last was a credible occupation for this quiet stranger.

'I'm going to tell the Colonel all about this,' I said. Delivett thought hard for several seconds, and put his bacon back on the fire.

'Well, sir,' he said, diffidently, 'if it's all the same to you, I'd much rather you made me Sanitary man.'

'Do you mean that you'd really like to go round with a bucket of chloride of lime, picking up tins and . . .'

'Yes, sir, I'd like that job.'

'You shall have it here and now. You are made Sanitary man for valour in the field, this very moment.'

In half an hour Delivett was walking round with a bucket, his head a little higher in the air, spitting a little more deliberately than before, as his new dignity demanded. He had found a vocation.

The signallers were always with the company, but never of it. They did no fatigues, they carried nothing but their leather-cased instruments and odd lengths of wire, they dug no trenches. They spent most of their time sitting down in dug-outs, buzzing their telephones, disappearing occasionally down a trench with one finger on a wire, following that wire round corners, across ditches and over fields. They were a clan within our tribe. Their dug-outs were, as a rule, close to the company headquarters, and day and night, when not actually telephoning, testing or signalling messages, they talked, they sang, and they whistled. At three o'clock in the morning, or just after standing down at dawn, when all the world was quiet, and an officer relieved from trench duty was trying to concentrate twelve hours sleep into the brief two hours allotted to him, a voice from the next dug-out rasped in a whining drawl:

'You left ba-hind a bro-ken do-oll.' . . . 'Beer emmer, beer emmer, beer emmer . . . 's that you, Bill?'

'I say, you remember that *estaminet* just beyond the cross-roads, well, I asked Madame . . .'

This was too much. I yelled out to them.

'Look here, you signallers, why can't you keep quiet? There are no messages coming through, are there?'

'No sir, we were only testing,' they replied.

'Well, shut up then, and let me go to sleep while the Boche is quiet.'

'Yes, sir.'

There was a dead silence for ten minutes, and

then a whispered conversation rising with the energy of contradictions into a full-flavoured argument about the price of coffee in that *estaminet*. I got up to attend to this.

'Why the hell can't you fellows keep quiet? Of all the damned chattering magpies I've ever come across, you are the worst.' I was angry, and much profanity followed, real hard cursing, of a sharp-edged variety that rises so easily to the lips in the early morning. I had lost an eighth part of my sleep, and nearly all my temper.

As I turned away from the door of their dug-out and went back to mine, I heard a cheery and unabashed voice saying quietly:

'Old Griff can't 'alf curse, can't he?'

After that there was silence.

We left the trenches and marched back to our billets at Riez Bailleul late on a summer night. There were many rumours, all of untraceable origin, that this was to be our last spell in the trenches for some time. Circumstantial evidence was freely put forward to prove each conflicting theory, quartermasters and post-corporals were fathered with definite statements of our ultimate destination that, had they been true, would have indicated a remarkable acquaintance with the minds of our commanders. We were content to know that we were going back to our quiet farmhouse in Riez Bailleul, and from the wild variety of forecasts we found enough material to justify the belief that the Division was to be relieved by another division in the same Corps.

The customary number of days in reserve went by with no sign of another visit to the trenches. Rumours sprang up again—we were going to Ypres, we were to join the Belgian Army, the French Army, the British forces near Arras, the Division was to be disbanded and remade into battalions of miners and tunnellers, into Engineers, into Pioneers, we were to go South to be trained for open warfare. Of all these tales, the truth was in the last surmise, and we were warned that the battalion would start on a long march to the South.

On our last evening in Riez Bailleul, the Sergeant-Major came to the Company Headquarters to say that the men were anxious to give a concert. A piano had been found, and for a small fee the owner was willing to allow us to take it to the orchard for the evening, provided we kept a tarpaulin over it to 'keep out the damp'. Would the officers come, and would I persuade the Adjutant to play the piano?

A man of undoubted administrative ability, with a knowledge of one half of the world of the day that made backwoodsmen of us all, added to a large acquaintance with its more prominent citizens, he had sauntered through many occupations before attaining a large measure of success as a journalist. Through all his varying moods there ran one thread that gave a continuity to his changeful personality, and that was his love of music. He was an attractive pianist, not of the highest order of technique, but endowed with a capacity to make others share in his own delight in playing. Yes, he would play, and he would accompany the songs.

We assembled in the orchard in the dusk, a hundred and fifty men lying about on the trodden grass, talking and smoking. A thin haze of tobacco smoke hung as a pale blue shadow against the darkening sky, and two candles in the piano sconces gave a round blur of yellow light. The air was still, and in the distance a rumble of far-off shell fire served as an echo to the thunder of a limbered wagon passing along the road. We sang a chorus or two to unstiffen the minds of all, to weld us into a unity of mood.

Some forms had been lashed together to make a precarious platform, and on this the Sergeant-Major, by virtue of his office, president and prime mover of such an enterprise, stood to announce that Corporal Jackson 'would oblige', following the time-honoured formula, by singing a song.

Corporal Jackson was greeted enthusiastically by all as he stepped up. At some time or another he had been on the stage, according to the best informed of the company—'made a lot of money in 'is day, 'e 'as, an' 'e carn't 'arf dance'. He walked across to the piano.

'Music?' said the Adjutant, with a smile.

'No sir, got no music.'

'What are you going to sing?'

' "Don't Stop Me", sir.'

'I don't know it—what's the tune?'

Jackson bent down and hummed into the Adjutant's ear.

'Right you are, Corporal. . . . Carry on.'

'Will you play a few bars of introduction first, sir, and then play the tune for the dance after each chorus?'

Corporal Jackson walked to the centre of the stage and gave an expert shuffle with his feet to test its stability. 'Mind them boots, Corporal, the Quarter's looking,' shouted some irrepressible member of the company.

It was a third-rate song, sung by a fourth-rate singer, followed by a second-rate clog dance, but in the remoteness of that green orchard in Flanders, far from any standard of comparison, it claimed and held approval for its own sake. The words of the chorus still remain, wedded to a jerky tune, both trailing an air of days long passed away:

> Don't stop me, don't stop me,
> I've got a little job to go to,
> 'Twas advertised in ninety-eight,
> If I'm not there I'll be too late. . . .

Another corporal, fat and tenorish, sang 'Thora', hanging precariously on its sentimental slopes, curving his mouth into a wonderful vowel fantasy over the

> Noightin-gales in the brenches,
> Stawrs in the mej-jic skoy.

A good hard-working Corporal, though his belt was a perpetual worry to him in his convexity.

But the evening grew to its grand climax when the stern-faced Sergeant-Major stood grimly on the stage, thin-lipped and hawk-eyed, to sing a ballad of Northern Lands. Every line in his face, and every contour in his spare body, gave the lie to his opening words:

> Oh, Oh, Oh, I'm an Eskimo,
> And I live in the Land of Snow. . . .

The rest of the song has faded, but that sense of contradiction is still vivid. He had to sing it twice because he could remember no other.

Private Walton hunched his shoulders and adjusted the weight of his body carefully from one leg to another until he found a position of stable equilibrium, mental as well as physical. From his pocket he pulled out a mouth-organ, wiped it carefully on the under-side of his sleeve, shook it and tapped it gently against his palm, presumably to remove any crumbs of tobacco or biscuit, and suddenly burst into a wild harmonic frenzy. From the welter of common chord and seventh there rose a recognizable tune, emphasized by the tapping of his foot, and he stimulated the whole company to song. When the audience had gathered sufficient momentum, he stopped to wipe his mouth-organ.

The next performer was Signaller Downs, who roused the community to a long-drawn-out sequence of 'Nev-vah Mind' in Gertie Gitana's undying song, a song that declined in speed as it grew in sentiment. The moon rose in the blue-grey sky, mellowing the darkness and deepening the shadows under the trees, turning the orchard into a fine setting for a nobler stirring of the spirit. Over the subdued chatter of many voices and the noise of an occasional lighting of a match came the silvery spray of notes from the piano. The Adjutant was playing quietly to himself, meditating in music. The talking ceased, and men turned away from their comrades to listen, until there was dead silence under the trees to make a background for the ripple of the piano.

The silence broke in upon the player and he removed his hands from the keyboard for an instant. The world seemed to plunge into a deep pool of silence, rising again to hear a supple cascade of showering notes as he played one of Debussy's *Arabesques*. When he finished there was a second or two of silence before the applause began, enough of a gap to show that his listeners had been travelling with him into another land. He played it again, and as he turned away from the piano he whispered to me, 'I told you that they could appreciate good music if they got the chance.' A summer night in an orchard, with a moon low in the sky, and in the heart of each man a longing—if music could not speak in such a setting it were not music.

SOUTH

In the morning we began our long trek South. We did not know our destination, nor the time we were to spend on our journey; as company officers it was enough for us to know the length of the day's march and where we were to sleep that night. For some reason unexplained to us, we marched through the heat of the June day, and after seven months of trench warfare we found the early stages troublesome until our feet were hardened. We spent a night at Merville, a town of good billets, and then two nights at a village called Gonnehem, a village rescued from oblivion by two memories, one of its fine old church, the other of its womenfolk—the dirtiest slatterns we had seen in France. Then up to the hills at Auchel, a mining village, with its men in blue smocks and leather hats, a long straggling street of indeterminate beginning and end.

After so many months in the plain it was good to stand on a hill. For fourteen days we had been out of the trenches, clean and comfortable;

body and mind were quickening again, early summer in the land, and a late spring inside us. The marching in good air was leaving its mark on us all, and we were gaining a release from the humiliating burden of mud that had clogged our pores and had turned our thoughts into its own greyness. We walked with a swing, we sang on the march; men began to laugh, to argue and even to quarrel, a sure sign of recovery from the torpor of winter. We were going into a battle, true enough, from which few of us could hope to return, but at the moment we were many miles from war, and the hedges were rich with dog-rose and honeysuckle; we were seeing the old flowers in new country.

This emancipation brought with it a re-kindling of our self-respect, showing itself in a more upright bearing, and in a shedding of the clod-hopping, farm labourers' shuffle of the feet, the last physical relic of the tyranny of mud. A month ago the Company was a disintegrated body of men, tired and dull, dragging the day into the night and the night into the day, with a horizon bounded on all sides by that damnable, evil-smelling and unnatural soil. Now we were above ground, welded into a free-moving unit, handling its arms with its old vigour and precision, no longer 'climbing up the rifle to the slope'. It was strangely easy to forget that this revival would be of short duration to most of us.

On our way out of Floringhem we found ourselves in a country of downs and wooded hills, small streams and high-hedged lanes—Hampshire again, and our first meeting with beauty in France. At one of our halts the officers were standing in a group in the road, smoking and talking, when the second-in-command of the battalion rode up to join us. After some desultory conversation about our last billets, he turned to me and said, 'By the way, I hear that you are going to another Brigade to be trained as a Staff Officer—many congratulations!' With this he rode away.

To me, these were words of liberation, they opened the door of my prison. Seven months of shelling, of mud, discomfort, and the deadening, unescapable routine of trench life, months of watching other men being killed and maimed, of dry-mouthed fear and racking fatigue; a time of waiting for the end, hoping that the end might be a bruising and not a sudden drop into darkness. All this weight of disharmony ran above one never-ceasing pedal note of 'No infantry officer can survive this war unless he is happily wounded.' Until this background is etched into the mind with the acid of experience, it is not possible to understand the full import of this message. For me, life had suddenly changed direction. Comparative safety, interesting work, a reasonable chance of survival without mutilation, and the elation that accompanied the knowledge that someone had chosen me to do something; the possibility of leave and of promotion, more pay and a richer housekeeping for my wife—this was the new country upon which I gazed through the suddenly opened door of my prison. A deep-lying thankfulness permeated the whole of my being, gaining strength from the knowledge that soon, very soon, the news would release some of the burden of anxiety that pressed down into a uniform greyness the days and nights of one whose life was linked to mine, who lived in daily dread of that baleful telegram from the War Office. A mad impulse came over me, not strange to one born in the mountains, to build a cairn on the roadside, marking the spot where I heard these words of freedom, but a whistle blew, and the battalion resumed the march down South. I was back in my Company, but with a difference.

When the mind has run riot for a few hours over the prospect of release and opportunity, there comes a certain pleasure in dwelling upon the greyer side of the picture. I was to go to another brigade as a stranger, possibly unwanted and half-suspected, to live day by day with a General, unable to conceal my ignorance, liable to be found out in a short space of time and returned to my battalion in disgrace. In a few days I would be turning my back on 'C' Company, on the men I lived with and loved, leaving them a little while before their great hour of trial, deserting them, in fact. So it was ordained, and for my betterment; I was to stand my trial, with no influence or authority over my judges, merely an infantry captain, temporary, with no relations or friends in high places, a man of no importance to powers military or civil. The reward of success was advancement in the army, and enough pay to lift me clear of the margin of anxiety here and at home; failure meant a reversion to the trenches, so there must be no tottering.

Several days passed before I received orders to go, days of some anxiety lest there should be a hitch in this fateful affair, but days of pleasant marching in country lanes, of long evenings in good billets in villages far removed from contact with the strident clash of war. The inhabitants of the cleanly kept cottages lived a life into which we could not enter. Our coming roused an excitement that died away with our going, and we never saw them at their daily struggle to prevent the army's intrusion from growing into an occupation. Farms, houses and inns undamaged by shell-fire suggested a prosperity and a strength alien to the provinces further North and East, but as we never penetrated into any intimacy with the villagers, we could not tell how they were faring.

My arrival at Brigade Headquarters created no stir. I had walked to the Château at Chelers, leaving my servant to bring my kit in the battalion cart. Never before had I entered a château, and there was a thrill in the thought of living in such magnificence. It was a newish house, standing in a small park, clean and white in the hot sunshine of June, decorated with a turret at every possible corner, and dominating the small village at its feet. It was half withdrawn from sight, yet eager not to be overlooked and ignored.

I met a soldier and asked him if this were the Brigade Headquarters, and I was somewhat taken aback when he said that it was not; it was the General's billet, and the Brigade office was in the small house near the church. I turned back, consoling myself for the loss of this magnificence by the confident hope that as the Brigade staff would be well housed, I should find myself in a good billet, even though it were not a château.

I entered the Brigade office and made myself known to an elderly Major sitting down at a table covered with papers. He said that the Brigade Major was on leave, and that he was merely deputizing for him; the Staff Captain would be in shortly and would find me a billet. When the Staff Captain arrived he extinguished all my expectations of comfort and dignity by announcing that I could sleep in a bell tent in the garden, as there was no billet to be had in the village. A little later we all walked to the château for tea, and I was introduced to the Brigadier. He said little, but whenever I looked in his direction I met his eye, and I felt that I was being assessed and valued. He was some sixty years of age, physically strong, with a hard and clear face, and the bearing of a man who has lived wisely. In the jargon of the day, he was a 'dug-out', a retired regular officer who had rejoined the army on the outbreak of war. The gossip of my old Brigade described him as a glutton for work, somewhat snappy in the early morning, sensible, and willing to listen even to a subaltern. At table he spoke as a man among men, and in my inexperience I found it hard to believe that he was a real General, own brother to the rest of his rank who walked the trenches in search of disappointment and of tasks undone, demanding an output of construction from tired men, wet and short of sleep, that would have staggered Henry Ford himself. He asked me no questions, but I felt that it was only because he had decided that there was no need to dissect a known specimen.

I spent the rest of the day in making myself as inconspicuous as possible, sitting in a corner of the office, reading orders and listening to the conversation of my companions, trying to penetrate unobtrusively into the life around me. It did not occur to me that as a Company Officer I had as much to impart to them as they had to teach me. In the evening I walked through the village and talked to some of the regimental officers I knew, keeping a watchful eye for my young brother, for his battalion was billeted in the village and belonged to my new brigade. I found him, and in his obvious delight at this turn for the better in my fortunes, I recovered some of my own, and conquered that feeling of utter loneliness and unimportance that assails every individual at the time of his first joining a strange unit. He was merely a boy who had come straight from school into the ranks, and it was a matter of pride to him that his brother should shine in the reflected glory of the Brigadier, as if he felt that things could not fail thereby to prosper.

After breakfast next morning the General asked me if I could ride. In sheer cowardice I said that I could, for I did not dare to begin my career by announcing my limitations. He told me to get the Machine Gun Officers' horse and to accompany him on a visit to the battalions at the training ground. My heart quailed within me when I saw a great black beast standing uneasily on the road, enormously tall, and as I thought, very fierce looking. I had neither spurs nor stick nor leggings, so I had tied my puttees cavalry-fashion. I clambered up on to the back of this unwilling creature, feeling extremely insecure at so great a height above the road. We started off, and to my good fortune, the General did not trot his horse. He questioned me about my experience and training, both in the ranks and as a commissioned officer, told me to learn everything that came my way, and to ask him questions about what I did not understand. He shook his rein and trotted, and I followed, taking great pains to keep behind him, as was fitting to my lower rank, and as my lack of horsemanship made essential if I were not to advertise my deficiencies.

I have no illusions whatever about my appearance on this occasion, but I take pride in having kept my seat. We rushed down the banks of sunken roads, and rushed up the other side, to the great danger of my nose; we jumped over trenches, and added to all my anxiety about my equilibrium was the determined effort to keep behind the General. When all was over and we reached Brigade Headquarters, the General turned to me and said, with a smile in his eyes:

'Next time I ask you whether you can do a thing, say so outright if you cannot.'

I answered timidly that, at any rate, I had not fallen off.

'No, but why you did not is more than I can say. . . . How much have you ridden?'

'This is the second time in my life I have ridden a horse, sir,' I replied.

'Good Lord, you might have broken your neck . . . don't do things like that again.'

When the day is divided between an attempt to conceal ignorance of the things that are common knowledge to your colleagues, and a struggle to acquire familiarity in unobtrusive fashion, dreading to make lack of learning, and the desire to learn, equally a source of embarrassment to others, the day passes quickly enough. I cannot say that I was taught to do anything, but there were ample opportunities for imitating others in what they did, and if questions were asked with a due regard for the niceties of time and place, they were answered. More than this could not be expected of men who worked hard enough, but had little gift or inducement to explain their daily tasks. With such men, all the world over, there is more to be earned from their negations than from their assertions.

To my fresh eye, the work was divisible into two categories—issuing orders, and seeing that those orders were carried out. In the nature of things, I had little to do with issuing orders, but enquiry into their fate and reminder of their existence seemed to involve a considerable running about. And here, as everywhere in the army, there was a fresh vocabulary to learn, a new craft jargon, another weapon of verbal equipment. The Staff Captain's activities were multifarious, and at first all but incomprehensible owing to my ignorance of the language. There was, and presumably still exists, a scheme of words and phrases that may be called a verbal shorthand for dealing on paper with matters as diverse as a court martial and a shortage of incinerators, an Esperanto of the army. How it arose is to me a mystery, but I can only surmise that someone once made an index, in alphabetical order, of all the commodities and occasions involved in war, and that the descriptive phrase in this index became a sacred title to be used henceforth and for ever in all writings. There is much to be said for the practice, as for a universal language, and the eye soon accustoms itself to 'Waggons, G.S.'. After a few weeks of army shopkeeping, the G.S. becomes a part of the waggon as integral as its wheels.

The British Army is, in some respects, an army of brothers, and every man above the rank of private is his brother's keeper. Every commander must know what his command is doing at the moment, and his superior officers must know what it did yesterday, and what it intends to do to-morrow. This concern, this anxiety, and interest, minute and unceasing, are as characteristic of the British Army as their non-existence is typical of other armies. It can be harassing, and it often is, but it is omnipresent throughout the hierarchy of the command

and the staff. A soldier, short of some article of equipment, mental or material, is a matter of concern to many functionaries far removed from contact with him. Private Smith, in a fit of temper, may by his delinquencies set in motion a long chain of Captains, Majors, Colonels and Generals, further removed from him geographically as they rise in rank, but all in some way concerned with his destiny.

VII

MAMETZ WOOD

MAMETZ WOOD

At seven in the morning, Brigade Headquarters was to 'close down' at one place and to 'open' at another. This has a sound of the impossible in it, but it is easily resolved into a problem of telephone communication. If there is a telephone at the new headquarters, giving a means of speech backward to Divisional Headquarters and forward to Battalion Headquarters, the command of the brigade can be as well exercised from the new hole in the ground as from the old. For in this war, a telephone wire was not only the outward sign of command, but the life-blood of its existence; a General without a telephone was to all practical purposes impotent, a lay figure dressed in uniform, deprived of eyes, arms and ears.

All through the night the signallers had worked at their task of picking and choosing the right wire from the tangled mass of tendrils that wound round post and trench in this desperate jungle, following the wire across country, testing it in sections, until the welcome sound of the right voice in response brought an end to their search. A chance shell, or the unlucky stumble of a passer-by, might cut the wire and send weary men out again on their search.

In the stuffy darkness of the old German dug-out an orderly lit a candle and roused us to say that it was half-past four. I swung my feet over the side of the wire-net mattress and stumbled up the stairs into the thin chill of the dawn, stupid and less than half awake, conscious chiefly of the difficulty of keeping my eyes from closing, and of a clammy, bitter-tasting thirst, a legacy from a short and too heavy sleep in a musty dug-out. Shivering and stretching, stamping my feet on the duckboards, swinging my arms like a cab-driver, I walked along towards the sound of a crackling wood fire and its promise of a cup of tea. There was an unnatural stillness in the air. No guns were firing, no transport moving. A thin column of smoke was rising slowly, twisting and swaying idly in the thin light. The whole world seemed to have slackened its pace to the merest saunter through the sky, with no perceptible disturbance of the morning air, without song of bird or step of man. A vague unreality had taken the place of the visible and audible environment, concealing all the muddle and horrors of the day before, revealing nothing but a sleeping shape stretching out over the chalky downs, blackening the light greenish-grey of the landscape.

As the light grew stronger, this straggling trail of black hardened into its distinguishable components; wagons, dumps of ammunition and stores, battery after battery of guns, big and small. A little below the dug-out, in the dip between it and the ground rising up towards Mametz, a string of guns squatted in a row, and from underneath a bivouac a gunner crept out, stretched himself, and walked through the line of guns to a stake in the ground. From this he removed a lamp. Other men followed him, appearing mysteriously from nowhere, and soon there was a bustle of life in this tiny village of nomads.

Far away to the South a shell burst in the empty air. Somewhere behind our hill a big gun fired, another followed it, and suddenly the battery below blasted a stuttering sentence of noises. The Devil had taken his seat at the keyboard to play the opening bars of his morning hymn; another day beginning, the last day for so many, a fine sunny day to devote to killing and bruising. Was it my last day? With a wise obstinacy, the mind refused to dwell on such a thought, and the signalman in my brain shunted such futile traffic into some siding, giving the right of way to the greater utility of a desire for a cup of tea. I found some biscuit and a tin of jam, and sat on an ammunition box near the fire, eating and drinking in silence. When I had finished I went down into the dug-out for my shaving tackle, and as I descended the steps into a crescendo of foul stuffiness I wondered how I had dared to sleep in such a cesspool of smells, and hurried back to the trench to shave.

When I came back to the fire I found Taylor, the Brigade Signalling Officer, seated on a box and drinking his cup of tea. He was a man of forty, quietly carrying about him a reserved air of authority and competence, unhurried in movement and in speech. The technical nature of his work preserved him from interference, and he ruled over his kingdom of men with a certainty of control denied to an infantry officer. No Brigadier could dispute with him concerning the wisdom or unwisdom of his dispositions of men or material. His duty was to give others a means of speech, and as he never failed in his task, his competency was obvious to all.

This morning his face was as grey as his hair, and his eyes were dull and tired. I greeted him and sat down by his side.

'When did you finish your job?' I asked him.

'I've just come from there now, and I'm going back with some more men as soon as they have had a bite of food. It's a long tramp from here to Pommiers Redoubt, and I lost my way coming back. . . . Lost two men on the job already!'

'Killed?' I asked.

'No, both wounded—shrapnel in the leg. I had a terrible job to get them away. We were out on a line across country and I couldn't find a battalion or anybody likely to have stretcher-bearers. I tied them up as well as I could and went out on a search. I left my torch with them in case I couldn't find my way back in the dark. Just as I was giving it up and going back to them, a gun went off near me, a blaze of light and a hell of a noise. I was down on my face before you could say 'knife', and I crept along till I got a bit nearer, and then I shouted. A gunner came out and yelled to me to come in quickly before they fired again. So I got some stretcher-bearers and got my lads away. Two good men, just when I most wanted them. Still, they are well out of it, poor devils, with a day like this in front of them.'

'What's it like at Pommiers Redoubt?' I asked.

'Just like any other hole in the ground. There's some heavy artillery headquarters there, and we may be glad of their lines before the day is out. . . . There's a lot of our fellows out there not buried yet. . . . You know old Evans the padre?'

'Yes, I know him.'

'I met him this morning, half an hour ago, just as it was getting light. He was going to do a bit of burying. I thought he looked queer . . . he was talking to himself, praying, may be, when I walked along with him. It was in North Wales Welsh, and I couldn't make much of it. I got talking to him, and I asked him why he was up so early. He said he hadn't been to bed. He went towards Fricourt yesterday evening looking for a grave. Someone you knew, said I. . . . Yes, my own boy's grave, said he.'

'Good God, I knew young Evans well—he was in the ranks with me,' I answered.

'Well, Evans, poor chap, had heard yesterday evening that his boy was killed near Fricourt the day before, so he went off at once to try to find his grave. He walked about for hours, but couldn't find any one who knew where it was, nor could he find the padre who buried him. He walked till he could walk no more, got a cup of tea from some gunners, and had a rest, and then walked back here. And now he's out again. Going to bury other people's boys, he said, since he couldn't find his own boy's grave to pray over. . . . What could you say? I left him to turn up to this place . . . my Welsh isn't very good, as you know, but I managed to say to him, "I'm not a soldier now, padre; I'm taking off my hat to you." And so I did, I took off my tin helmet. . . . You couldn't talk English to a man who had lost his boy. . . .'

'No . . . not to a Welshman,' I replied.

'But there's a man for you, Griff . . . off to bury other men's boys at five in the morning, and maybe his own son not buried yet, a couple of miles away. There was some shrapnel overhead, but I saw him going up the slope as if he were alone in the world. If I come through this bloody business, I'd like to go to that man's church. The only thing he said that I could make out was that bit of a Welsh hymn—you'll know it, the one they sing at funerals to that tune that curdles your blood worse than the Dead March. . . . Well, this is no time to be talking of funerals, I'm going back to Pommiers Redoubt—are you coming with me?'

'I might as well,' I replied, 'I'm doing nothing here, but I'd better ask the Brigade Major first, in case he wants me.'

The Brigade Major, after some years in the East, was not at his best in the early morning, and in the minimum of words, told me that I could go.

Taylor was stuffing some biscuits into his haversack when I came back to him.

'You'd better do the same,' he said. 'You never know where you might land up to-day.'

'Cheer up, Taylor,' I answered. 'There are so many of us about to-day that you and I might well be booked for a through trip.'

I cut off a hunk of cheese and put it in my haversack with some biscuits, and filled my water-bottle: pipe, tobacco, matches, maps, note-book, orders—I made sure that these were on or about me.

We set off up the hill, passing the grey and red ruins of Mametz village on our left as we walked up towards Pommiers Redoubt. The guns were firing, and an occasional shell-burst crashed through the air with a venomous answer. Transport was crawling about in the distance, small groups of men were moving, dark against the white gashes in the chalk. Scattered equipment lying about underfoot, tangles of wire, small dumps of forgotten stores, all left behind in the advance. Other things were left behind in the advance, part of the purchase price of this downland, grim disfigured corpses rotting in the sun, so horrible in their discolour that it called for an act of faith to believe that these were once men, young men, sent to this degradation by their fellow men. One thought ran in and out of the mind like a shuttle in a loom; any one of the thousands of seconds in this July day might reduce Taylor or myself into a like travesty of living man, useless lumber best thrown away near some such heap of rubble as Mametz, 'where Ruin calls his brother Death'. There was some comfort in the thought that my wife did not know that this day held for me any fuller measure of danger than any other day of war, that for her there was no greater straining of the tense string that ran from hope to fear. And if I were killed, I would turn from man to memory in her heart without leaving a mutilated shell of flesh to haunt her eyes.

'I haven't seen anything of my young brother for some days,' I said to Taylor. 'I wonder what he is doing. He's such a kid, for all his uniform. He ought to be still in school, not in this bloody shambles.'

'He's all right,' replied Taylor. 'I saw him last night. The brigade called for two runners from each battalion, and he came as one of them—

he's somewhere near that old German dug-out we came from.'

'I wish I'd known. It was his birthday two days ago, and I've got a little present for him in my valise. I wonder if he'll ever see another birthday. . . . I don't know how I could face my mother if anything happened to him and I got through.'

'Well, he's got a chance, Griff—he might be in the line. What do you think of our job to-day?'

'The General was cursing last night at his orders. He said that only a madman could have issued them. He called the Divisional Staff a lot of plumbers, herring-gutted at that. He argued at the time, and asked for some control over the artillery that is going to cover us, but he got nothing out of them. We are not allowed to attack at dawn; we must wait for the show at Contalmaison, well away on our left.'

'We'll get a good view of that show from Pommiers Redoubt.'

'I dare say, but don't you think that it is a funny thing to keep us waiting in the lobby? We are going to attack Mametz Wood from one side, and Contalmaison is on the other side of the Wood—why shouldn't both attacks be made at the same time? It would spread out the German fire.'

'I suppose it would spread out ours too,' said Taylor, 'but if you are going to start asking "Why" about orders you'll soon be off the Staff or off your head. You might as well say, "Why attack the Wood at all?" '

'But I do say that, Taylor. Look at it now—it's a forest. What damage can our guns do to that place? If you had a good dug-out near the edge of that wood, and a machine-gun, how many men would you allow to cross that slope leading up to the Wood? You'd mow them down as soon as they stood up.'

We had reached the high ground at Pommiers Redoubt, and, standing in a trench, scanning the Wood with our glasses, it seemed as thick as a virgin forest. There was no sign of life in it, no one could say whether it concealed ten thousand men or ten machine guns. Its edges were clean cut, as far as the eye could see, and the ground between us and the Wood was bare of any cover. Our men were assembled in trenches above a dip in the ground, and from these they were to advance, descend into the hollow, and cross the bare slope in the teeth of the machine-gunners in the Wood. On their right, as they advanced across the bullet-swept zone, they would be exposed to enfilade fire, for the direction of their advance was nearly parallel to the German trenches towards Bazentin, and it would be folly to suppose that the German machine-guns were not sited to sweep that slope leading to the Wood.

'I'm not surprised that the General cursed when he got his orders,' said Taylor. 'The truth about the Brigadier is that he's got too much sense. He was soldiering when some of the fellows above him were still playing marbles. I'm going to see my signallers. . . . I'll see you later.'

A little further along the trench a group of officers were engaged in a discussion over a map spread out on a box. I went up to speak to them, and found that this was the headquarters of a group of Heavy Artillery concerned in the bombardment of Contalmaison, and about to wipe it off the map, as I gathered.

Taylor came up out of a dug-out. 'We're through to the old Brigade Headquarters, the Division, and to the battalions. How long we'll be through to the battalions is another story,' he said.

The General arrived with the Brigade Major and the Staff Captain, looked around him quickly, and turned to me.

'Have you found a good place for us?'

'Yes sir, there's room in the signallers' dug-out, but this is a good place for seeing.'

'It's close on seven o'clock. Are we through to everybody, and have the battalions reported that they are in position?' he asked.

'Yes sir.'

'Then send out the report that Brigade Headquarters has opened here. You stay with me, and be ready to take down any orders or messages when the time comes.'

With this he went to consult with the Brigade Major. I stood on a step in the side of the trench, studying the country to the East and identifying the various features from the map. Our guns were quiet, and, although everybody within sight was moving, there was a weird stillness in the air, a brooding menace. Why was I standing here when men I knew were lined up in readiness to expose their bodies to a driving sleet of lead? The thought of the days' torment, doomed, as I thought, from its beginning, to bring no recompense, weighed like a burden of iron. The sound of a heavy bombardment, some distance away to our left, broke in upon the silence and grew to a storm of noise and smoke. Contalmaison was the target, prominent upon a hill until the smoke obscured the hill-top, turning it into a dark cloud hung between a blue sky and brown-pitted earth. Out of this cloud, at intervals of some minutes, an orange sheet of flame made an effort to escape, only to be conquered and smudged out by the all-pervading smoke. It did not seem possible that there could be guns enough in France to create such a fury as this, and my mind went back to the artillery fire of 1915 and early 1916. Our trench bombardments were things of no importance when contrasted with this, and I felt half ashamed to remember that they had frightened me.

At eight o'clock the artillery began its bombardment of the edge of Mametz Wood. A thousand yards away from where I stood, our two battalions were waiting. I read the orders again. The attack was to be carried out in three stages, beginning at half-past eight, reaching in succession three positions inside the Wood, under the protection of an artillery barrage. Smoke screens were to be formed here and there. Everything sounded so simple and easy.

A few minutes after eight, all our telephone wires to the battalions were cut by the enemy's reply to our fire. There was no smoke screen, for some reason never explained—perhaps someone forgot about it. This was the first departure from the simplicity of the printed word. Messages came through, a steady trickle of runners bringing evil news; our fire had not masked the German machine-guns in Mametz Wood, nor in the wood near Bazentin. The elaborate time-table suddenly became a thing of no meaning, as unrelated to our condition as one of Napoleon's orders; our artillery barrage was advancing in mockery of our failure, for we were two hundred yards away from the Wood.

A message arrived from the Division. In twenty minutes' time, the artillery would begin another bombardment of the edge of the Wood, and under cover of this we were to renew the attack—in twenty minutes. We were a thousand yards away from the battalions, with no telephone communication; there were maps at Divisional Headquarters, they knew where we were, they knew where the battalions were, and they knew that our lines were cut. A simple sum in arithmetic. . . . Our operation was isolated; no one was attacking on either flank of our Brigade, so that there was complete freedom of choice as to time. With all the hours of the clock to choose from, some master-mind must needs select the only hour to be avoided. He did not ask himself whether the order could reach its ultimate destination in time . . . the answer to that sum in arithmetic.

Every attempt to move near the Wood was met by a burst of frontal and enfilade machine-gun fire. Shells were falling, taking a steady toll of lives. Later, another order came from Divisional Headquarters. We were to attack again, to make a third effort to penetrate this wall of lead. The General gave some orders to his Brigade-Major, called me to accompany him, and we set out for Caterpillar Wood and to reach the battalions. Although the day was fine, the heavy rains of the preceding days had turned the chalky soil into a stiff glue. The hurry in our minds accentuated the slowness of our progress, and I felt as if some physical force was dragging me back. Haste meant a fall into a shell hole, for we had abandoned the attempt to move along the trench. Shrapnel was bursting overhead, and a patter of machine-gun bullets spat through the air. We passed through Caterpillar Wood, and in a disused trench on our left I saw an Artillery officer. I turned off to ask him whether his telephone was working, and learned that he was in communication with a Heavy Artillery Group somewhere beyond Pommiers Redoubt. I ran down the trench to rejoin the General, and we dropped down the bank into the nullah between Caterpillar Wood and Mametz Wood, passing a stream of 'walking wounded' making their way out.

There was a dug-out in the bank, with scores of stretchers down on the ground in front, each stretcher occupied by a fellow creature, maimed and in pain. This was the Advance Dressing Station; twenty rounds of shrapnel would have made stretchers unnecessary. Along the bare ridge rising up to Mametz Wood our men were burrowing into the ground with their entrenching tools, seeking whatever cover they might make. A few shells were falling, surprisingly few. Wounded men were crawling back from the ridge, men were crawling forward with ammunition. No attack could succeed over such ground as this, swept from front and side by machine-guns at short range. Down in the nullah we were out of sight of the enemy, but fifteen minutes of shrapnel would have reduced the brigade to a battalion, and every minute that passed seemed to bring nearer the hour of our inevitable annihilation. We were caught in a trap, unable to advance, unable to withdraw without being observed. It must ever remain one of the many mysteries of the War why the enemy did not pound us with shell fire, for this was so obviously the only place of assembly.

The time was drawing near for the renewal of the attack, for another useless slaughter.

Casualties in officers had been extremely heavy, and the battalions were somewhat disorganized.

'This is sheer lunacy,' said the General. 'I've tried all day to stop it. We could creep up to the edge of the Wood by night and rush it in the morning, but they won't listen to me. . . . It breaks my heart to see all this.'

'If I could get you through on the telephone, would you talk to them again?' I asked.

'Of course I would, but all the wires are cut, and there is no time to go back.'

'I know of a telephone to an Artillery Group, and they might get you through to the Division,' I answered.

'Find out at once whether I can get through,' he replied.

I hurried up to the trench where I had seen the Artillery officer and found that his wires were still uncut, and as I ran back to the General I prayed in my heart that they would hold; the lives of some hundreds of men depended upon it. It did not occur to me that words sent along that wire might fail in their object, that someone sitting far away would look at a map and say, 'No, you must reach that Wood at all costs.' Seen in its stark reality, our position was so hopeless that a dispassionate account of it must convince any one, even at a distance of six miles, that to remain where we were would be no less calamitous than to try to advance. The enemy had shown no desire to hold that exposed ridge with men, for his bullets were defence enough, and in a short space of time his artillery must realize that there was a magnificent target in that hollow between the ridge and the bank.

When I came back to the hollow, I could not find the General. I ran from one group of men to another, working my way up the ridge, until I found him organizing the defence of the position against any possible counter-attack. Shells did not seem to matter; my whole existence, up to that very minute, had been of no importance to the world, but my original conversation with that Artillery officer, so obviously prompted by what men call Destiny, could lead to the saving of hundreds of lives, and must not fail to do so. I knew that I had been 'chosen' for this. Ten minutes later I sat in the trench while the General spoke on the telephone, tersely describing the utter folly of any course of action other than a gradual withdrawal under cover of outposts, and quoting figures of our casualties. He was arguing with determination. There was opposition, but he won. As I jumped up to start on our way back to the ridge, he stopped me.

'Wait a minute. They are shelling this bank,

and this message must get through. Give me a sheet of paper,' said he. He wrote down his order for the withdrawal and gave it to me. 'You go one way, and I'll go another way. Join me in the hollow. Go as fast as you can.' With this he went down the trench, and I ran and stumbled down the bank, still feeling perfectly safe in the hands of Destiny.

Two hours later the General and I were dragging our way from the nullah and back towards Pommiers Redoubt. We sat down in a trench to let a file of men pass by, and I suddenly noticed that his face was grey and drawn.

'Have you eaten anything since this morning?' I asked him.

'No . . . have you?' he replied. 'I feel whacked.'

'Will you wait here a few minutes—I'll be back soon,' I said.

I had seen a dug-out, and I went inside it. Some signallers were lighting a fire to boil a mess-tin full of water; they lent me an enamel cup, and in it I put a tablet of compressed tea. The brew was strong and the water was not boiling, but it was a warm drink, and I took it back to the General. It revived him, and we munched our biscuits as we walked along.

Back again to Pommiers Redoubt, but with a difference, in the flat greyness of approaching dusk. The noise of the guns had died down to a sullen scale-practice, with an occasional, and almost accidental chord, so different from the crashes of the day. Stretcher-bearers, bowed forward under their straps, were carrying their burdens of suffering across the ploughed and pitted slopes.

'How did you come to find that telephone?' asked the General.

'I happened to notice the Artillery officer on my way down, and I went to ask him if his line back was working. Don't you remember my leaving you?'

'No, I don't remember. . . . Well, it saved the lives of some hundreds of men, but it has put an end to me.'

'Why do you say that?'

'I spoke my mind about the whole business . . . you heard me. They wanted us to press on at all costs, talked about determination, and suggested that I didn't realize the importance of the operation. As good as told me that I was tired and didn't want to tackle the job. Difficult to judge on the spot, they said! As if the whole trouble hadn't arisen because someone found it so easy to judge when he was six miles away and had never seen the country, and couldn't read a map. You mark my words, they'll send me home for this: they want butchers, not brigadiers. They'll remember now that I told them, before we began, that the attack could not succeed unless the machine guns were masked. I shall be in England in a month.'

He had saved the Brigade from annihilation. That the rescue, in terms of men, was no more than a respite of days was no fault of his, for there is no saving of life in war until the eleventh hour of the last day is drawing to an end. It was nearly midnight when we heard that the last of our men had withdrawn from that ridge and valley, leaving the ground empty, save for the bodies of those who had to fall to prove to our command that machine guns can defend a bare slope. Six weeks later the General went home.

The next day brought no time for crying over spilt milk. The Staff Captain had become a casualty, and had been evacuated as a shell-shock case, so that it fell to my lot to do his work, poorly equipped as I was for the task. For the first time I realized that, battle or no battle, reports must be made, returns prepared, and administrative work must continue as if we were all in barracks. I did my best, but if there are lacunæ in the statistics, memoranda 'lost' and unanswered, mine must be the blame. The General and the Brigade Major were so concerned with matters of war that I could not in very shame intrude upon their consultations to ask advice on questions that appeared to me to lack fundamental importance. On paper, I promised where I did not perform, and, over the telephone, parried all demands from the Division.

The two remaining brigades of the Division were to attack Mametz Wood in the afternoon of the following day, and we were to be in reserve, ready to take over the defence of the wood if the attack succeeded. This venture was differently staged. A narrower front gave promise of greater support from the artillery, and the approach, bad as it was, did not make success impossible. Until we were called upon to fight, the brigade was to spend its time carrying and working for the others, in spite of our exhaustion in numbers and in strength. At the last moment, the attack was postponed for twelve hours, and it was not until dawn on the 10th July that the flower of young Wales stood up to the machine-guns, with a success that astonished all who knew the ground. Two of our battalions had become involved in the fighting in the Wood, and at five o'clock in the afternoon, our brigade was ordered to relieve the attacking brigades and to take over the responsibility for the defence of the sector against any counter-attacks. It was five o'clock in the morning before this relief was completed.

A little before dawn, the General and the Brigade Major went up to the Wood, leaving me to follow them at midday. At seven in the morning, as I was wrestling with some papers that I did not understand, a runner came in with a message from the General. The Brigade Major had been wounded, and I was to go up at once to join the General in the Wood. This, at any rate, was a man's job, and I left the papers in their disarray. A month ago, my military horizon was bounded by the limits of a company of infantry; now I was to be both Brigade Major and Staff Captain to a Brigadier-General in the middle of a battle. I consoled myself with the thought that if I could originate nothing, I could do what I was told to do.

I passed through two barrages before I reached the Wood, one aimed at the body, and the other at the mind. The enemy was shelling the approach from the South with some determination, but I was fortunate enough to escape injury and to pass on to an ordeal ever greater. Men of my old battalion were lying dead on the ground in great profusion. They wore a yellow badge on their sleeves, and without this distinguishing mark, it would have been impossible to recognize the remains of many of them. I felt that I had run away.

Before the Division had attempted to capture Mametz Wood, it was known that the undergrowth in it was so dense that it was all but impossible to move through it. Through the middle of the Wood a narow ride ran to a communication trench leading to the German main Second Line of defence in front of Bazentin, a strong trench system permitting of a quick reinforcement of the garrison of the Wood. With equal facility, the Wood could be evacuated by the enemy and shelled, as it was not part of the trench system.

My first acquaintance with the stubborn nature of the undergrowth came when I attempted to leave the main ride to escape a heavy shelling. I could not push a way through it, and I had to return to the ride. Years of neglect had turned the Wood into a formidable barrier, a mile deep. Heavy shelling of the Southern end had beaten down some of the young growth, but it had also thrown trees and large branches into a barricade. Equipment, ammunition, rolls of barbed wire, tins of food, gas-helmets and rifles were lying about everywhere. There were more corpses than men, but there were worse sights than corpses. Limbs and mutilated trunks, here and there a detached head, forming splashes of red against the green leaves, and, as in advertisement of the horror of our way of life and death, and of our crucifixion of youth, one tree held in its branches a leg, with its torn flesh hanging down over a spray of leaf.

Each bursting shell reverberated in a roll of thunder echoing through the Wood, and the acid fumes lingered between the trees. The sun was shining strongly overhead, unseen by us, but felt in its effort to pierce through the curtain of leaves. After passing through that charnel house at the southern end, with its sickly air of corruption, the smell of fresh earth and of crushed bark grew into complete domination, as clean to the senses as the other was foul. So tenacious in these matters is memory that I can never encounter the smell of cut green timber without resurrecting the vision of the tree that flaunted a human limb. A message was now on its way to some quiet village in Wales, to a grey farmhouse on the slope of a hill running down to Cardigan Bay, or to a miner's cottage in a South Wales valley, a word of death, incapable, in this late century of the Christian Era, of association with this manner of killing. That the sun could shine on this mad cruelty and on the quiet peace of an upland tarn near Snowdon, at what we call the same instant of Time, threw a doubt upon all meaning in words. Death was warped from a thing of sadness into a screaming horror, not content with stealing life from its shell, but trampling in lunatic fury upon the rifled cabinet we call a corpse.

There are times when fear drops below the threshold of the mind; never beyond recall, but far enough from the instant to become a background. Moments of great exaltation, of tremendous physical exertion, when activity can dominate over all rivals in the mind, the times of exhaustion that follow these great moments; these are, as I knew from the teachings of the months gone by, occasions of release from the governance of fear. As I hurried along the ride in this nightmare wood, stepping round the bodies clustered about the shell holes, here and there helping a wounded man to clamber over a fallen tree trunk, falling flat on my face when the whistle of an approaching shell grew into a shrieking 'YOU', aimed at my ear, to paralyse before it killed, then stumbling on again through a cloud of bitter smoke, I learned that there was another way of making fear a thing of small account.

It was life rather than death that faded away into the distance, as I grew into a state of not-thinking, not-feeling, not-seeing. I moved past trees, past other things; men passed by me, carrying other men, some crying, some cursing, some silent. They were all shadows, and I was no greater than they. Living or dead, all were unreal. Balanced uneasily on the knife-edge between utter oblivion and this temporary not-knowing, it seemed a little matter whether I were destined to go forward to death or to come back to life. Past and future were equidistant and unattainable, throwing no bridge of desire across the gap that separated me both from my remembered self and from all that I had hoped to grasp. I walked as on a mountain in a mist, seeing neither sky above nor valley beneath, lost to all sense of far or near, up or down, either in time or space. I saw no precipice, and so I feared none.

Thus it was that the passing seconds dealt a sequence of hammer-blows, at first so poignantly sharp that the mind recoiled in unbelief, but in their deadly repetition dulling the power of response and reaction into a blind acceptance of this tragedy, and in the merciful end, pounding all sensibility into an atrophy that refused to link sight to thought. A swirl of mist within me had thrown a curtain to conceal the chasm of fear, and I walked on unheeding and unexpectant.

I reached a cross-ride in the Wood where four lanes broadened into a confused patch of destruction. Fallen trees, shell holes, a hurriedly dug trench beginning and ending in an uncertain manner, abandoned rifles, broken branches with their sagging leaves, an unopened box of ammunition, sandbags half-filled with bombs, a derelict machine-gun propping up the head of an immobile figure in uniform, with a belt of ammunition drooping from the breech into a pile of red-stained earth—this is the livery of War. Shells were falling, over and short, near and wide, to show that somewhere over the hill a gunner was playing the part of blind fate for all who walked past this well-marked spot. Here, in the struggle between bursting iron and growing timber, iron had triumphed and trampled over an uneven circle some forty yards in diameter. Against the surrounding wall of thick greenery, the earth showed red and fresh, lit by the clean sunlight, and the splintered tree-trunks shone with a damp whiteness, but the green curtains beyond could conceal nothing of greater horror than the disorder revealed in this clearing.

Even now, after all these years, this round ring of man-made hell bursts into my vision, elbowing into an infinity of distance the wall of my room, dwarfing into nothingness objects we call real. Blue sky above, a band of green trees, and a ploughed graveyard in which living men moved worm-like in and out of sight; three men digging a trench, thigh-deep in the red soil, digging their own graves, as it chanced, for a bursting shell turned their shelter into a tomb; two signallers crouched in a large shell hole, waiting for a summons to move, but bearing in their patient and tired inactivity the look of dead men ready to rise at the trump of a Last Judgment.

Other memories steal upon the screen of vision, growing imperceptibly from a dim remembrance of a part into a firmly-built unity of composition as the eye gains control over its focussing, but this image of war in its brutality flashes in an instant, sharp and clear in its uttermost detail. Then, at its first seeing, it was unreal, unrelated to my past, for the mist was within me, but now and for ever it must rise with every closing of my eyes into a stabbing reality that governs the future. So many things are seen more clearly now that the passing years have allowed the mud of action to settle at the bottom of the pool of life.

Near the edge of this ring I saw a group of officers. The Brigadier was talking to one of his battalion commanders, and Taylor, the Signals officer, was arguing with the Intelligence officer about the position on the map of two German machine-guns. The map itself was a sign of the shrinking of our world into a small compass: a sheet of foolscap paper bearing nothing but a large scale plan of Mametz Wood, with capital letters to identify its many corners, was chart enough for our adventure this day. 'What has happened to the Brigadier?' I asked Taylor. 'Why is his arm in a sling?'

'Shrapnel,' he answered. 'He got hit as he was coming up to the Wood, but he got the doctor to dress it for him. He says it doesn't hurt him, but I expect it will before the day is over.'

'Did you see the Brigade Major . . . was he badly hit?'

'Shrapnel in the leg—his gammy leg. The stretcher-bearers took him away, cursing everybody and damning his luck. Seems to me he doesn't know luck when he sees it. You'll have to get down to it now.'

'Yes. Tell me what has happened so far.'

'You never saw such a mess. Nobody knows where anybody is, the other brigades are still here—what's left of them—all mixed up.'

'Are your lines holding? Are you through to anybody?'

'Devil a soul,' answered Taylor. 'As soon as I mend a line the Boche breaks it. You can't keep a line up with that barrage across the bottom of the Wood. There's an artillery F.O.O. just behind you, in that shell hole; I don't know what the devil he's doing up here—he can't see twenty yards in front of him, and all his lines are gone. He might as well be in Cardiff.'

As soon as the battalion commander had gone I joined the Brigadier.

'Is this the Brigade Headquarters?' I asked.

'It is,' he replied. 'It's an unhealthy place, but we've got to be somewhere where we can be found by night as well as by day. Get your notebook and take down the position of affairs at the moment. We have been sent here to take over the line and to make secure against counter-attacks. There are four battalions of our brigade, and what is left of four other battalions. We are holding an irregular line about three hundred yards from the end of the Wood, bending back towards the West. The units are very mixed up, and I've just come back from trying to give them their boundaries. They are all straightening themselves out and digging in, but the undergrowth is so dense that it will be some hours before they are in their proper places.'

'Are we supposed to attack and clear the Wood?'

'No. Our orders last night were to take over the line. I've told the battalion commanders to reconnoitre and to push out where they can. We don't know whether the enemy is holding the far end in any great strength.'

'If we have to attack later on, how do you propose to do it?'

'By surprise,' answered the General. 'With the bayonet only. That's the only way to get through the Wood. If our artillery will keep quiet, we can do it. Here's my map—make a summary of what I've told you. It took me hours to get round our line.'

Runners came from the battalions giving news of progress in consolidation, and reporting that the enemy was in considerable strength on the Northern edge, with plenty of machine-guns. I sat down on a fallen tree-trunk and made a report of the situation, read it over to the General, and went in search of a runner to take it to the Division. Taylor was standing by a large shell hole, talking to his signallers.

'How can I get this to the Division?' I asked.

'Give it to me: that's my job. I've got a telephone down at Queen's Nullah, and if a runner can get out of the Wood and through the barrage, the message gets through.'

'Are the runners getting through?'

'Some don't, and some of those that do don't get back. . . . Don't give me any messages that are not absolutely essential and urgent. I'm getting short of men—seven down already this morning. I don't know what it will be like when the Boche wakes up. He's got us taped here. Look at those cross-rides—did you ever see such a butcher's shop?'

At this moment a signaller orderly came up to deliver a message. I opened it, glanced through it, and took it to the General. His face hardened as he read it. The Divisional Commander informed us that the enemy's trenches in front of Bazentin were being shelled, and that it was quite impossible that he had any strong force in Mametz Wood. The brigade was to attack and occupy the Northern and Western edges of the Wood at the earliest possible moment. Indeed, the Corps Commander strongly impressed the importance of clearing the Wood without delay.

While we were digesting this order, and drafting new orders to the battalions, a Staff Officer came up to join us. His red and black arm-band showed that he came from Army Headquarters, and he spoke with all the prestige native to a traveller from distant lands who had penetrated to within a few hundred yards of the enemy. He brought orders that we were to carry out an attack upon the two edges of the Wood. The Brigadier listened to him with the patience of an older man coldly assessing the enthusiasm of youth. When the Staff Officer had finished, the General spoke.

'I've just had orders from the Division to attack and clear the rest of the Wood, and to do it at once. The defence is incomplete, the units are disorganized, and I did not propose to attack until we were in a better position. My patrols report that the Northern edge is strongly held. I haven't a fresh battalion, and no one can say what is the strength of any unit.'

'What do you propose to do?' asked the Staff Officer.

'My intention is to take the remainder of the Wood by surprise, with the bayonet if possible; no artillery bombardment to tell him that we are coming. I want a bombardment of the main German second line when we have taken our objective, to break up any counter-attack. Do you know anything about the artillery programme?'

'No, I do not. Are you in communication with the Division or with any of the artillery groups?'

'No, except by runner, and that takes a long time. I'm issuing orders to the battalions to get ready to advance quietly at three o'clock, and I'm sending a copy of the order to the Division; if you are going back will you get in touch with them as soon as possible and tell them that I don't want a barrage?'

The Staff Officer left us, and we worked at the orders for the battalions. The enemy was shelling the Wood, searching it, as the gunners say, and there were intermittent bursts of machine-gun fire, with an occasional uneven and untidy rush of rifle fire. On our right a few bombs burst in a flat, cracking thud. At a quarter to three, while we were waiting for the hour, a sudden storm of shells passed over our heads, bursting in the Wood some two hundred yards ahead of us.

'Good God,' said the General. 'That's our artillery putting a barrage right on top of our battalion! How can we stop this? Send a runner down at once . . . send two or three by different routes . . . write the message down.'

Three men went off with the message, each by a different way, with orders to get to Queen's Nullah somehow or other. Our barrage had roused the enemy, and from every direction shells were falling in the Wood; behind us a devilish storm of noise showed that a heavy price must be paid for every attempt to leave the Wood.

The Brigadier sat on a tree-trunk, head on hand, to all appearances neither seeing nor hearing the shells.

'This is the end of everything . . . sheer stupidity. I wonder if there is an order that never reached me . . . but that Staff Officer ought to have known the artillery programme for the day. And if there is another order, they ought not to have put down that barrage until they got my acknowledgement. How can we attack after our own barrage has ploughed its way through us? What good can a barrage do in a wood like this?'

At twenty past three our own artillery was still pouring shells into the wood. None of the runners had returned. Taylor sent three more to try to rescue us from this double fire, but ten minutes later we were left with no worse burden than the enemy's shelling. Reports came through from the battalions that we had suffered severely. As the afternoon drew out into the evening, we nibbled away here and there with fluctuating fortune, but at the approach of night the enemy reinforced his line and kept us from the edge while he pounded away with his artillery.

It was nearing dusk when Taylor came up to me.

'I want to have a word with you,' he said, drawing me away. 'I've got bad news for you. . . .'

'What's happened to my young brother . . . is he hit?'

'You know the last message you sent out to try to stop the barrage . . . well, he was one of the runners that took it. He hasn't come back. . . . He got his message through all right, and on his way back through the barrage he was hit. His mate was wounded by the shell that killed your brother . . . he told another runner to tell us.'

'My God . . . he's lying out there now, Taylor!'

'No, old man . . . he's gone.'

'Yes . . . yes, he's gone.'

'I'm sorry . . . I had to send him, you know.'

'Yes, of course . . . you had to. I can't leave this place. . . . I suppose there's no doubt about his being killed?'

'None—he's out of it all now.'

So I had sent him to his death, bearing a message from my own hand, in an endeavour to save other men's brothers; three thoughts that followed one another in unending sequence, a wheel revolving within my brain, expanding until it touched the boundaries of knowing and feeling. They did not gain in truth from repetition, nor did they reach the understanding. The swirl of mist refused to move.

Within the unclouded portion of my being a host of small things took their place on the stage, drawing their share of attention, and passing on. More orders to draft, situation reports to send out, demands for more bombs, enemy trench-mortars to be shelled into silence, machine-guns wanted by everybody. The General put his hand on my shoulder. It began to grow dark. An order came from the Division to say that we would be relieved that night by a brigade from another Division, and that on completion of the relief we were to return to our bivouacs. More orders to the battalions. The wheel was still revolving, while the procession of mere events moved without a break.

I walked towards the large shell hole that served as a shelter for the signallers, carrying in my hand a sheaf of messages for delivery. From the background of bursting shells came a whistle, deepening into a menace, and I flung myself on my face. I remembered a momentary flash of regret that I was still two yards from the protection of that shell hole. A black noise covered everything. When my eyes opened I was lying on my back, further away from the hole. I got up on my hands and knees and crawled to the signallers, still clutching the crumpled messages, and spoke to them. There was no answer. The rim of another large shell hole nearly touched their shelter, and the three signallers were huddled together, dead, killed by the concussion, for there was no mark of a wound.

The wheel came to rest, and I do not remember much of what happened afterwards. The night came, within and without. I have a clear memory of walking up the ride towards the battalions, of tripping over a branch, and of a flash of anger because I hurt my shoulder when I fell. The General went forward to one battalion to make sure that the line was securely held to cover the relief, and I went to another battalion on the same errand. The night seemed to pass in a black film, broken only by the flashes of bursting shells. I am told that I found the battalion.

Some time later, a heavy storm of shell fire drove me into a little trench where I crouched with some men to shelter. We talked in Welsh, for they were Anglesey folk; one was a young boy, and after a thunderous crash in our ears he began to cry out for his mother, in a thin boyish voice, '*mam, mam. . . .*' I woke up and pushed my way to him, fumbling in my pockets for my torch, and pulled him down to the bottom of the trench. He said that his arm was hurt. A corporal came to my assistance and we pulled off his tunic to examine his arm. He had not been hit, but he was frightened, still crying quietly. Suddenly he started again, screaming for his mother, with a wail that seemed older than the world, in the darkness of that night. The men began to mutter uneasily. We shook him, cursed at him, threatening even to kill him if he did not stop. He did not understand our words, but the shaking brought him back. He demanded his rifle and his steel helmet, and sat in the bottom of the trench to wait for the relief, talking rationally but slowly. English voices came out of the dark, enquiring for another battalion of our brigade; more men stumbled by in search of the posts they were to relieve. Our time was drawing to an end.

Dawn was breaking when I reached the clearing. The General had been waiting for me; another wave had passed over our brigade, and all the men of our battalions who were destined to leave the Wood were now on their way down to the bivouacs. He looked at me and asked me if I would like to sit down to rest, but I wanted to go on. We picked our way over the fallen timber and round the corpses, some sprawling stiffly, some huddled against the splintered tree-trunks, until we were clear of the Wood. I was afraid to look closely at them, lest I should recognize one of them.

Below the Wood, the enemy was still maintaining a barrage, but we were too tired to hurry. Our field-guns were pushing up towards the slopes, some were in position and were firing to support the attack on the German second line. With them was another brother of mine, a bombardier, but I did not know it. We walked in silence, until the General asked me if I had any food. I found some biscuits in my haversack, and realized that I had not eaten for twenty-four hours.

It was eight o'clock when we reached the old German dug-out and drank a cup of tea. As we were finishing, a Staff Officer from the Division arrived to tell us that we were to get ready to move at short notice. Protest was useless; the battalions must be clear of the bivouacking ground by five o'clock the next morning, and we must march a distance of fourteen miles to another sector of the front.

The day passed in getting ready for the march, and in trying to write a letter to my father and mother to tell them what had happened. When at last I succeeded, I felt in some queer way that an episode was ended, that all feeling had been crushed out of existence within me. Night came, but I could not sleep. At two in the morning we set out to join the battalions, and as dawn was breaking over Bazentin, I turned towards the green shape of Mametz Wood and shuddered in a farewell to one, and to many. I had not even buried him, nor was his grave ever found.

VIII

THE GLEANING

THE GLEANING

It was early in the morning of a fine day in July. The clear air and fresh sunlight, the green fields, the white road and the pale blue sky all combined together to make a fit setting for a pageant of youth in bright colours. There was a quality in the hour and the place, a harmony in the open countryside, indescribable save in terms of serenity. Nature stood still, poised securely in a major key, unrelated to the life of man and unconcerned with his discords. Against this background of freshness and purity a slow-moving worm of dingy yellow twisted itself round the corner made by a jutting shoulder of the downland. The battalions of the brigade were marching in column of fours along the road, and from a little distance it was clear that there was a lack of spine in the column. No ring of feet, no swing of shoulder, no sway of company; slack knees and frequent hitching of packs, a doddering rise and fall of heads, and much leaning forward. Fatigue and exhaustion in a body of men attain an intensity greater than the simple sum of all the individual burdens of its members warrant. This loss of quality in a unit marching away from the Somme battlefield was made more evident by the rising memory of the sturdy column that swung its way down the hedge-bound lanes in the early mornings of the end of June, a bare fortnight past, singing and laughing in the happiness of relief from the fetters of the trenches in Flanders. To-day the silence was unbroken, save by the shuffling of feet and the clanking of equipment.

The intensity with which we had striven to attune the mind to a soldier's way of thinking, to the cultivation of a quick and semi-instinctive assessing of military worth, showed itself in this first impact. Here was a weapon, all but shattered on so rough usage, fallen in quality from a spear-head into a ploughshare, fit only to turn the soil and to revert to a quiet pre-occupation with the tenancy of a sector where war played at husbandry. Back to the digging of trenches, to the daily struggle against the fall of earth, to the assiduous draining of water; no other verdict was possible. It did not seem necessary to give exact shape to thought, to translate into words the inner meaning of this decay; to look at the column, to turn away and to look again, was exercise enough to leave an abiding sense of pain.

Gradually, and almost imperceptibly, the mind ceased to dwell upon this impression of decline. The habit of being a soldier was but newly acquired, and the power of concentrating upon the narrower military importance of the phenomenon had not completely overlaid the older endowments of life and upbringing. Our future use became a thing of less moment than our present helplessness. The weight of tired limbs and a dragging pack, the burning blows of a hard road upon swollen feet, the inescapable burden of a rifle, the pull of an ammunition pouch upon a sore shoulder, the reiterated blows of a water-bottle—these, and a thousand other pains, sounded clearly through the air, drowning the note of serenity rising from the green country-side.

A walk along the column brought a new aspect of our condition into view. A captain was leading a battalion, subalterns and company sergeant-majors were marching at the heads of companies, corporals in front of platoons. Men were marching abreast who had never before stood together in the same file. There are no gaps in a battalion on the march, though many have fallen, but the closing-up that follows losses tells its own tale. The faces of many silent and hard-eyed men showed that they were but half-aware of their new neighbours, newcomers who jostled the ghosts of old companions, usurpers who were themselves struggling against the same griefs and longings, marching forward with minds that looked backwards into time and space.

The long-stretched agony of the week had scoured something out of every man in the column. Experience had added nothing to our inheritance, for the days were spent in an endeavour to hold something of what we possessed, in a stern defence of the outposts of the soul. Man had fought against the tiger, no less than with his fellow man, against the overwhelming terror of sudden fear as implacably as he fought against danger. There had been no victory, no triumph. Eyes were dull and slow-moving, coated with a film that turned their opacity into a revelation of all the anguish that lay behind them. Who has not met the dumb protest in the stare of such eyes, lingering even into the days of peace?

Suddenly a turn of the mind brought to light another measure of our state. The four battalions marching up from the Somme made a column but little longer than the span of one battalion on the way down: we had left behind us nearly two thousand men of our brigade. The measure of our condition was the measure of the price paid for Mametz Wood; the largest of the woods in the Somme battlefield had reduced a strong division to a shadow. In the capture of this obstacle to our advancing line we had discharged our immediate task, only to be ourselves flung aside as of little worth.

We did not ask whether the reward were equal to the sacrifice; it may be that there is no equality in such matters, that war is the very negation of all value. Confined as we were in a world governed by a force operating ruthlessly in one direction, there was a wall on either side of our path. All that could happen to us was, at the whim of this force, a quicker or slower progress along our narrow alley, lacking knowledge of our destination, impotent to control our motion. We could not know whether our destination would prove to be our Destiny, nor was it given to us to glance over the walls at other ways of climbing the hill. This is not to say that our attitude was one of fatalism; when one may not look to the right and left, there still remains another dimension. If resistance were of no avail, non-acceptance sprang up within us all as a natural reaction against the method of our employment. It was not so much that we admitted our inability to gauge the need for such a task; we did not even doubt that the capture of Mametz Wood was an indispensable operation, we imagined no Evil Fate choosing us as a weapon.

It would be untrue to suggest that our discontent rose up against the existence of a Battle of the Somme, or that we rebelled inwardly at the likelihood of another experience of this nature. There was no discussion about the relative merits of rival methods of attack or of alternative fronts. Although our lives were the letters that went to its spelling, the word Strategy was never on our lips. We held no opinion on such high matters, but the generosity with which we disclaimed knowledge of so large a territory of the world of soldiering heightened the confidence, amounting almost to arrogance, of our condemnation of certain practices then in high favour with our superiors.

To every one of us it was bitterly clear that wars could not be won by piling up corpses in front of machine-guns. Shell-fire was inevitable, and its dangers were fair risks of war, but when one line of men had failed to satiate the hunger of machine-guns, there was nothing inevitable in sending forth another wave to destruction. The argument was not vitiated by isolated instances of success here and there, at a price never quoted. Nor indeed was there anything of the inevitable in a constant failure to link up the loose threads of intention scattered over the battlefield, an omission that was made catastrophically evident to us in the gap that divorced artillery support from infantry action.

These were the thoughts that built up a weight of dissatisfaction, dragging at our heels day and night, clogging all power to eliminate the needless tortures of battle. All war was bad, but the thinking of our masters made it worse: wrong was in the saddle, all the world over. If we had devoted our lives to the study of war, this inward revolt against the method of our governance in the field might have risen clear of vagueness into a definite plea for another way of war-thinking, but we were neither civilians nor soldiers. We had lost the layman's power of judging between the rival theories of experts, without capturing the acquiescent confidence of a soldier. All the counsel we could give amounted to little more than a cry of 'Not thus . . . not thus.'

Added to the burden of fatigue and grief, we were governed by a dark feeling of personal failure. Mametz Wood was taken, but not by us, it seemed; we were the rejected of Destiny, men whose services were not required. The dead were the chosen, and Fate had forgotten us in its eager clutching at the men who fell; they were the richer prize. They captured Mametz Wood, and in it they lie.